T0265603

Monika Künti

Weaving *with* Strips

SCHIFFER PUBLISHING

4880 Lower Valley Road • Atglen, PA 19310

PHOTOGRAPHS BY SAMUEL KÜNTI

MONIKA KÜNTI

Weaving *with* Strips

18 Projects That Reflect the Craft,
History, and Culture of Strip Weaving

Dedication
For Noémi Speiser and Therese Leutwyler and for all the good, helpful spirits in museums everywhere in the world.

Copyright © 2022 by Schiffer Publishing, Ltd.
Originally published as Aus Streifen geflochten by Monika Künti
©2019 Haupt Verlag, Bern, Switzerland
Translated from German by Simulingua, Inc.

Library of Congress Control Number: 2021942408

All rights reserved. No part of this work may be reproduced or used in any form or by any means—graphic, electronic, or mechanical, including photocopying or information storage and retrieval systems—without written permission from the publisher.

The scanning, uploading, and distribution of this book or any part thereof via the Internet or any other means without the permission of the publisher is illegal and punishable by law. Please purchase only authorized editions and do not participate in or encourage the electronic piracy of copyrighted materials.

"Schiffer," "Schiffer Publishing, Ltd.," and the pen and inkwell logo are registered trademarks of Schiffer Publishing, Ltd.

Photographs, unless otherwise stated: Samuel Künti, Bern, Switzerland
Layout: Christina Diwold, Linz, Austria
Type set in Minion Pro/Roboto

ISBN: 978-0-7643-6323-8
Printed in China

Published by Schiffer Publishing, Ltd.
4880 Lower Valley Road
Atglen, PA 19310
Phone: (610) 593-1777; Fax: (610) 593-2002
Email: Info@schifferbooks.com
Web: www.schifferbooks.com

For our complete selection of fine books on this and related subjects, please visit our website at www.schifferbooks.com. You may also write for a free catalog.

Schiffer Publishing's titles are available at special discounts for bulk purchases for sales promotions or premiums. Special editions, including personalized covers, corporate imprints, and excerpts, can be created in large quantities for special needs. For more information, contact the publisher.

We are always looking for people to write books on new and related subjects. If you have an idea for a book, please contact us at proposals@schifferbooks.com.

Other Schiffer Books on Related Subjects:
Basketry Basics: Create 18 Beautiful Baskets as You Learn the Craft, BJ Crawford, ISBN 978-0-7643-5745-9
Earth Basketry, 2nd Edition: Weaving Containers with Nature's Materials, Osma Gallinger Tod, ISBN 978-0-7643-5343-7
Rooted, Revived, Reinvented: Basketry in America, Kristin Schwein & Josephine Stealey, ISBN 978-0-7643-5373-4

Contents

Introduction 8

History, Materials, and Social Aspects 10

Origins of Weaving Techniques 12

How Basketry Is Used 15

    Collecting and Carrying 15

    Storage 18

    Traveling and Packing 20

    Building and Living 21

    Games and Rituals 24

    Clothing and Jewelry 25

    Weaving Connects 29

General Information 32

Terms and Definitions 34

Materials 41

    General Remarks 41

    Preparing Plant Materials 42

    Preparing Paper 43

    Materials That Work Well for Cutting into Strips 44

    Sourcing Materials 44

    External Form of the Weaving Materials 45

Tools and Aids 46

    Tools 46

    Aids 46

Working the Materials 48

Creative Potential 52

    Dimensions 52

01

02

03

The Character of the Structure..52

Patterns and Decorations 53

Hanging or Setting Up...54

Reinforcing 55

Carrying Devices 56

Adding 57

Gather, Compress, Fold, Roll Up 59

Practice and In-Depth Tasks 60

Make Mistakes...60

Techniques
....62

Introduction to Techniques..64

General Information about This Book 65

Notes on the Instructions 65

Shedding 66

Securing the Weave...66

Technique Group 1—Starting a Project and Constructing a Surface 68

Starting from the Center with Loose Weaving

Elements and Shedding 70

Starting from the Center to Make a Circular Surface 74

Starting from the Center with Loose Weaving Elements

in Three Directions (Open) 78

Starting from the Center with Loose Weaving

Elements in Four Directions 82

Starting along a Line..84

Starting with Groups of Weaving Elements 110

Starting over a Solid Form..115

Technique Group 2—Edges or Rims and Finished Edges....................116

Linear Finished Edges..119

Zigzag Finished Edges...123

Finished Edges with Extra Elements 127

Freestyle Edges 130

Technique Group 3—Three-Dimensional Objects 132

Orthogonally Woven Objects 134

Diagonally Woven Objects 144

Objects Woven in Three Directions 166

Enclosed Three-Dimensional Objects 168

Patterns And Decorations 176

Two Groups of Patterns and Decorations 177

Structural Patterns 178

    Twill Patterns 178

Patterns with Colored Weaving Elements 186

Patterns and Decorations Applied after Weaving 188

Conclusion 191

The Pictograms and Their Meaning 192

Appendix 194

Sources 194

Index 199

About the Author 200

Acknowledgements 200

04

05

Introduction

Library books and work samples

I love
doing
what I
can't do
yet.

I would have liked to have had a book like this my-self when I started to study weaving techniques intensively about a quarter of a century ago.

In the Museum der Kulturen Basel (Museum of Cultures), in addition to the then-permanent exhibition on the "Classification of Textile Techniques," there were two large departments that were central for my learning: Oceania and South America. Objects woven from strips exerted a great attraction for me. Unfortunately, I could not find any books of instructions or courses on this subject anywhere. So I did what the textile designer Jack Lenor Larsen did, when he said: "I love doing what I can't do yet!"—an intense phase began, which I like to call my "self-taught teaching and traveling years."

Later, I got to know and value Noémi Speiser. She became my learning companion, and my self-study took shape. In addition to experimenting, systematic thinking became increasingly important. Soon the question was posed as to whether I should continue my at-one-time-interrupted ethnology studies and later specialize in weaving techniques, or whether—even at an advanced age—I could do an apprenticeship as a basket weaver.

In fact, it is actually still possible to learn this trade today, and so it came to be that I was allowed to apprentice myself to Therese Leutwyler for three years. Therese is a passionate third-generation basket maker, and I was in the best of hands for learning this wonderful handicraft from scratch.

During that time, I realized how exploitative world trade and working conditions in low-wage countries are—how else could all those baskets and

furniture be offered to us for so little money? Basketry is actually a pure handicraft: one element after the other is shaped together to create a weight-bearing and cleverly constructed design—work processes that inspire me anew, again and again!

In 2003, I set up my own workshop in a really beautiful studio in the Old Town of Bern. An exciting and fulfilling time began: researching techniques from outside Europe, producing European-style basketry handicrafts, repairing workpieces, designing new ones, exhibiting, teaching and drinking tea—my workshop offered the perfect setting for all of this. In my own "handwriting," I created countless basket objects from natural materials, mats made of paper, woven rag rugs, and works for exhibitions and competitions, as well as materials for courses and my first book*.

In the exhibition "StrohGold" ("Straw Gold") in the Museum der Kulturen Basel: I'm exhibiting where it all started! Dialogue of two mats woven using the same technique, the one an artfully printed original from Vanuatu (pandanus), and the other a work of mine (100% paper). Photo: Derek Li Wan Po, Museum der Kulturen Basel

Being able to write this book is a wonderful way to continue my work. I like to share what I have discovered—a bit also with the intention of infecting others with my enthusiasm, to open their eyes to the beauty of basketry so that they might get the desire to put a hand to it themselves. Thus, this book becomes an invitation to immerse yourself in the marvelous possibilities of constructing amazing structures out of simple strips.

Wishing you happy creative work,
Monika Künti

Freestyle basket bowl by Monika Künti, rattan reed bast.

* Einhängen & Verschlingen: Maschenbildung mit Vorangeführtem Fadenende (Interlink & Intertwine Making Stitches with the Leading End of the Thread), Haupt, 2014

History,

Materi

Social A

ls, and

spects

History, Materials, and Social Aspects

A bird as a virtuoso basket weaver.
© Ingo Arndt Photography

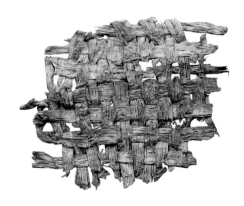

Woven piece from Meilen, Switzerland—
Feldmeilen-Vorderfeld (Zurich),
orthogonally woven, oak bast. Photo:
Kantonsarchäologie Zurich, Martin
Bachmann, taken in a 1:2 scale

Origins of Weaving Techniques

It's impossible to say exactly by whom, when, and where each kind of woven piece was invented. Increasing mobility in the course of human history (migration of peoples, sea voyages, colonization, missionary work, etc.) has enabled and promoted the spread of weaving techniques and the exchange of knowledge and skills. But even without being able to prove direct contact among cultures, many weaving techniques have developed in the same or similar ways on several continents.

Weaving techniques are among mankind's oldest cultural techniques. People have always needed containers to collect, carry, or store something. Inspiration for these containers can be found in natural models, such as bird nests or the intertwined parts of plants. The development of techniques was directly related to the materials available—each continent, each region, each culture had different materials that were suitable for weaving.

Textiles (which also include basketry), unlike objects made of stone, clay, metal, or glass, can be made from easily perishable materials. This means that they will not last forever unless they have been preserved under special circumstances (such as being contained in ice, sand, salt, or boggy soils). The oldest known finds are several thousand years old and come from ancient and early historical periods.

What makes weaving techniques unique is the fact that nowadays people are still weaving the base for a willow basket or a mat from palm leaves, just as their ancestors did thousands of years ago. The basic features of materials and techniques have remained the same. To weave, you need

Straw plaiting made on simple machines. View of a machine room in the hat-weaving industry, the Bruiser company, around 1910. Photo: Strohmuseum im Park, Wohlen, Aargau, Switzerland

hardly any tools or aids except your hands. And with few exceptions (chair caning, wire mesh, narrow straw plaits), basketry can still not be manufactured industrially. Rather, in contrast to pottery or woodturning, it's not possible to replace humans with machines in basketry—even today, every basket in the world is completely handmade!

All this indicates that weaving was an outstanding civilizational achievement for humankind. Collecting, transporting, storing, designing, discarding, constructing, counting, assigning, calculating, building up from individual parts, forming patterns, knowing materials, marketing—these are just a few of the key words that are directly associated with weaving.

Weaving techniques require attention and coordination of intellect and body. Your body sways along with the movements, you use rhythmic repetitions, and you get haptic experiences. The individual work steps are learned and practiced from the simple to the complex; you can adjust the degree of difficulty individually. Once you have mastered the basic skills, a great sense of calm can disseminate when doing this work.

Basketry techniques are incredibly diverse. No other group of textile techniques has such a wide range of materials, techniques, shapes, and functions. It is simply impossible to list all of these in full.

Basketry
techniques
are
incredibly
diverse.

In Maumere, northeast of Flores, Indonesia, Pak Goa weaves a traditional basket of palm leaves for daily transport of items to the market. Photo: Margrit Linder

How Basketry Is Used

The objects presented below are intended not only to illustrate the diversity and beauty of basketry, but also to illustrate its outstanding technical properties such as elasticity, flexibility, stability, and lightness.

COLLECTING AND CARRYING

Baskets work very well for collecting and transporting; they are available in an infinite variety. You can carry them in your hand, on your arm, on your back, on your shoulders, or on your head.

Instant Baskets

This is what I call the containers that are made in no time out of locally found materials. These baskets serve, for example, to transport harvested products or live animals and are, so to speak, disposable packaging that is used only for a short time and disposed of again after use. Such objects are now also popular souvenir items for tourists.

The finished basket in use at the market in Maumere, northeast of Flores. Photo: Margrit Linder

Transport basket for market, open three-directional weave. Photo: Christine Zbinden

Handle Baskets, Basket-Weave Bags, Backpack Baskets
There is a large selection in this category.

Handle basket made of chestnut woodchip, orthogonally woven

Swing or frame basket. Photo: H. Brauer

Shopping basket from Paraguay, orthogonally woven

Fruit basket from the Mediterranean, woodchip, orthogonally woven

Tanzanian basket-weave bag, palm leaf, diagonally woven, twill pattern

Handle basket for the table, metal, orthogonally woven

16

Anjat, Dayak Kenyah carrying basket made of rattan, Setulang, North Kalimantan, Indonesia. Photo: Margrit Linder

Dayak Lundayeh women harvesting forest vegetables, using diagonally woven baskets of bamboo, rattan, and red acrylic paint, Long Layu, Krayan, North Kalimantan, Indonesia. Photo: Margrit Linder

Reproduction of a carrying ring seen in a museum

Carrying Rings

These rings have always fascinated me; in many cultures, they are used to support heavily loaded baskets that are carried on the head. The rings are woven over a firm base.

Baskets used for storage can be found in all shapes, of all materials and weaving techniques, in all cultures all around the world.

STORAGE

There is scarcely anything that cannot be stored in a woven container. Storage baskets can be found in all shapes, of all materials and weaving techniques, in all cultures around the world. In making them, the weavers demonstrate their skills in using design vocabulary, materials, and technique. They use sophisticated considerations to determine how a basket should fulfill certain functions. A storage basket can, for example, be set on feet so that no moisture can penetrate the stored goods. Or you can apply a layer of lacquer to protect it from moisture.

Variations: of covered baskets, bamboo, diagonally woven, twill pattern, Laos

ase with cover, bamboo, diagonally woven, will pattern, Laos

Basket bowl covered with lacquered paper (now flaking off), bamboo, dragon's blood (resin), diagonally woven, twill pattern, Japan

Series of miniature covered baskets, palm leaf, diagonally woven, Southeast Asia

at basket bowl, peeled willow, orthogonally oven, twill pattern, fine weaving technique

Small basket with plaited rim, New Zealand flax, diagonally woven, New Zealand

Storage basket, diagonally woven, rattan, alimantan, Indonesia

ox with lid with many special details, agonally woven

Decorated box with lid, woven in three directions

Flat bowl, birch bark, diagonally woven

Woven bands used or making sails, Alamy, Photo Resource Hawaii

TRAVELING AND PACKING

Sails

The most impressive examples I know of woven strips are the woven sails used on Polynesian outrigger boats. These made it possible to traverse incredibly long distances across the seas. The large-sized sails were sewn together from individual narrow bands. Both the sailing technique and the way the sails are made are still maintained today for special occasions, for example, in Hawaii.

Boats

Other unusual examples are round boats, woven from bamboo and sealed with resin. You can find such shuttle, rescue, and coastal boats in the coastal regions of Vietnam.

Packing Materials

Due to its lightness, high impact resistance, and general availability, basketwork has always been an attractive material for packing. For example, basketwork products from the Far East, sewn into large mats, have traveled far. And porcelain from China came to Europe in woven protective cases. Even today, basketwork is used as packaging—thus, for example, I throw away the packaging for my favorite tea, made from palm leaf strips—which is a shame!

Sailboat from Tonga. Drawn by William Hodges, engraved by W. Watts. Alexander Turnbull Library, Wikimedia Commons, PD

Bamboo round boat, Vietnam. Photo: Christine Zbinden

Mat as packaging material for straw plaiting from China

Palm leaf packaging for tea, woven, lined with cardboard

BUILDING AND LIVING

Building Materials

Basketwork is also used for building and construction. Basketry techniques are used to build bridges, fences, walls, and so forth.

Construction work at the Centre Pompidou-Metz. Photo: Mossot, Wikimedia Commons CC-SA-3.0

Toilet huts in Vietnam. Photo: Christine Zbinden

Bamboo bridge over the Loboc River in the province of Bohol, the Philippines. Paul Lewin, Wikimedia Commons CC-SA-2.0

Detail of house wall. Photo: Alamy Stock, image BROKER

Working on an orthogonally woven mat to make a house wall. Photo: Alamy Stock, Rob Walls

Installation of 21 PET lamps,
Eperara-Siapidara Collection,
Colombia. Photo © ACdO

Ayam mat in the Baloy Adat of Pagun
Labuk, an assembly hall of the Dayak
Agabag, 15.4 x 2 meters, Tanjung
Lang-sat, North Kalimantan, Indonesia.
Photo: Margrit Linder

Living

In central Europe, basketry is mainly used to make seating furniture and lamps. Classics such as the Thonet company chairs and the B35 armchair designed by Marcel Breuer feature woven rattan seats.

So-called lounge furniture—prefabricated frames covered with machine-woven plastic—is particularly in vogue. But this has little to do with traditional basketry handicrafts anymore.

In many countries, mats used as a floor covering, for wall cladding, for room dividers, or for seating and sleeping pads are still very common fittings and fixtures for living interiors. Bamboo, rattan, palm leaf, or pandanus are used to make the strips for weaving.

Mat for floor covering, diagonally
woven, twill pattern, Vietnam

Household and Kitchen

In addition to carrying and storage, baskets are used as woven shelf baskets and wastepaper baskets, planters, place mats, bread and fruit baskets, sieves, presses, fly swatters, insect screen baskets, fans, plates, containers, coasters, key rings, etc.

The Southeast Asian rice dish called ketupat, cooked in interwoven young coconut leaves. Photo: Alamy, 500px

Sieves and plate baskets, orthogonally woven, twill pattern, baskets at center and right from Paraguay

Cheese press, esparto grass (made in strips), diagonally woven, twill pattern, Spain

Fan, diagonally plaited from palm fronds, twill pattern, Paraguay

Place mats and coasters made using various techniques and materials

Wastepaper basket made from willow splints

Manioc press from the museum pedagogical collection, Museum der Kulturen, Basel, palm leaf, diagonally woven, twill pattern

Detail of manioc press

23

Balls, tightly woven in three
directions, rattan, Laos

GAMES AND RITUALS

Toys

Basketwork is not just useful; you can also have a lot of fun playing and passing the time with basketwork items. These items are quickly made and easy to replace if worn out. Did you get to know Frobel stars (Advent stars) or mobiles made of woven fish during your childhood? Toys are woven together in Polynesia in exactly the same way!

In Thailand, children play a ball game called "sepak takraw," which uses artfully woven balls made of rattan.

In many countries, children play with tubelike objects known as finger traps. Your finger gets stuck in the finger trap, and the basketwork closes tightly around your finger when you try to pull your hand away—instead of releasing your finger as you expected.

Finger trap from Japan

Ritual Objects

The use of woven objects in ceremonies or at recurring festivals is still common in many cultures today.

Giraffe, diagonally woven, straw

Making decorative woven objects, Bali. Photo:
Christian Muehlethaler

Decorative basketwork in the shape of a
dragon, diagonally woven, palm leaf, Bali.
Photo: Christian Muehlethaler

CLOTHING AND JEWELRY

Mats as Clothing Material

In Indonesia, Southeast Asia, and Polynesia, people wear mats on their body like clothing during certain festivals. This has always made a big impression on me—how can structures be woven to be so pliant that they almost drape like woven fabrics?

My favorite item is a "dress mat" from Tonga, which was brought to England in the 18th century by one of James Cook's expeditions. I saw this beautiful piece for the first time in 2011 at an exhibition at the Historisches Museum (Historical Museum) of Bern. What mastery lies behind this plumed structure!

Vala dress mat from Tonga, 18th century, © Ethnological Collection of the Georg-August-University Göttingen (Oz 143). Photo: Harry Haase

Hats, Bags, Belts, and Shoes

Woven hats, bags, or shoes have been around since prehistoric times. Along with the traditional materials such as leather, straw, bast or inner bark, or palm leaf, there are the more modern ones such as cellophane, raffia viscose, paper, or plastics.

Hats are an inexhaustible topic. It is hard to believe how many techniques and materials are used to make headgear! Until the middle of the 20th century, there was even a flourishing hat-weaving industry in Switzerland, in the Freiamt region of Aargau. These hats have made a triumphant procession around the world. In the Strohmuseum im Park (Straw Museum) in Wohlen (Canton Aargau), this chapter of cultural history is recounted wonderfully.

The most famous woven hat is probably the Panama hat—contrary to its name, it is woven in Ecuador. This product is still manufactured today in masterful quality from very fine so-called toquilla straw.

View into a specialist shop for hat supplies, Berlin 1910. Photo: Strohmuseum im Park, Wohlen Aargau

Straw plaiting at home, Canton Aargau, around 1910. Photo: Strohmuseum im Park, Wohlen Aargau

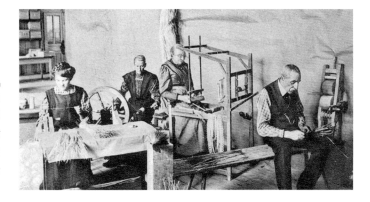

Hat bodies ("blanks" for making hats), diagonally woven, twill pattern, natural and synthetic materials

Group of hats from Southeast Asia, palm lcaf, bamboo

Leather belt, diagonally woven, Italy

Small shoulder bag, twill and satin weave

Group of pouches and bags, diagonally woven, twill pattern, pandanus, Solomon Islands

Artfully patterned shoulder bag made by the "Fashion from the Forest" project, rattan, diagonally woven, twill pattern

Handbag, diagonally woven, New Zealand flax, New Zealand

Panama hats.
Photo: Sarah Stierch,
Wikimedia Commons
CC-SA-4.0

Jewelry

The versatility of weaving techniques has always been appreciated for making jewelry—a playground for creative minds in the past as well as today!

Decorative buttons

Bracelets, very fine willow splints, different techniques, Germany

Bracelets and finger rings, orthogonally woven, Argentina

Working together and learning: Ibu Dormia, Ibu Polena, Ibu Salina, Ibu Martina—Agabag weavers in a training workshop 2010 in Tanjung Langsat, North Kalimantan, Indonesia. Photo: Margrit Linder

Showing each other how it works: Ibu Dormia shows Ibu Linting how to start an orthogonally woven base for a bag; underneath: an Agabag people's ayam mat, rattan, naturally dyed, Tanjung Langsat, North Kalimantan, Indonesia. Photo: Margrit Linder

Reing and tayen baskets as well as the Lungaye people's raung basung hats in a shop in Long Bawan, Kerayan, North Kalimantan, Indonesia. Photo: Margrit Linder

Weaving Connects

Weavers are highly regarded in many cultures and are considered to be guardians of important know-how and traditions. Patterns that tell complex and beautiful stories are passed down from generation to generation. Fortunately, there are projects that are committed to trying to prevent the impending disappearance of basketry handicrafts. For example, Margrit Linder uses her photographs to document a project in Indonesia. Under the title "Fashion from the Forest," rattan products from North Kalimantan are being manufactured and sold under fair-trade conditions. The focus is on preserving and passing on traditional basketry handicrafts and adapting them to the demand on the international market. In this way, indigenous women are earning a regular income and keeping this handicraft and the knowledge about harvesting the raw materials alive.

Detail of an Agabag mat made of rattan, naturally dyed, pattern: tiningo'ulun, Tanjung Langsat, North Kalimantan, Indonesia. Photo: Margrit Linder

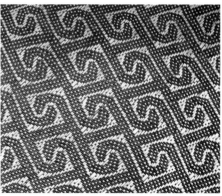

Detail of an Agabag mat made of rattan, naturally dyed, pattern: sinangau, Tanjung Langsat, North Kalimantan, Indonesia. Photo: Margrit Linder

Ayam mats, bags, and budui baskets made by the Agabag people, Tanjung Langsat, North Kalimantan, Indonesia. Photo: Margrit Linder

Project week in a school class: community mat, poster paper, diagonally woven. Photo: Peter Santschi

Weaving connects. This can be seen everywhere where people create basketry—be it when weaving in a communal setting, when working with weaving techniques in art and science, or in teaching. In order to weave in a social way, it is not even necessary to speak the same language.

Mathematicians, chemists, biologists, and other scientists work with weaving-like structures and patterns—in the microcosm as well as in the macrocosm. For example, Franz R. Schmid has been researching pentagonal lattice structures for years, analyzing and reconstructing them and making artistic representations.

I am concluding this "tour" with the memory of an exhibition of folk art from Latin America—which had the wonderful title of "Design without Designer"—that I saw in Langenthal, Switzerland, years ago. A text about the exhibition included the following lines by Valentin Jaquet:

In its own way, folk art is also a popular "matter of course." Its perfect forms of use, whose beauty is not just based on functionality, can certainly be compared to the creative work of the designer. From time immemorial, folk art has inspired creation by designers, not to mention that it has copied often and unabashedly.

Since then, I have no longer been making judgmental differentiations among design, craftsmanship, applied art, and art. Cultural creators from around the world create interesting things, day after day. Look, marvel, appreciate, and talk to others about it—this is something we should be doing!

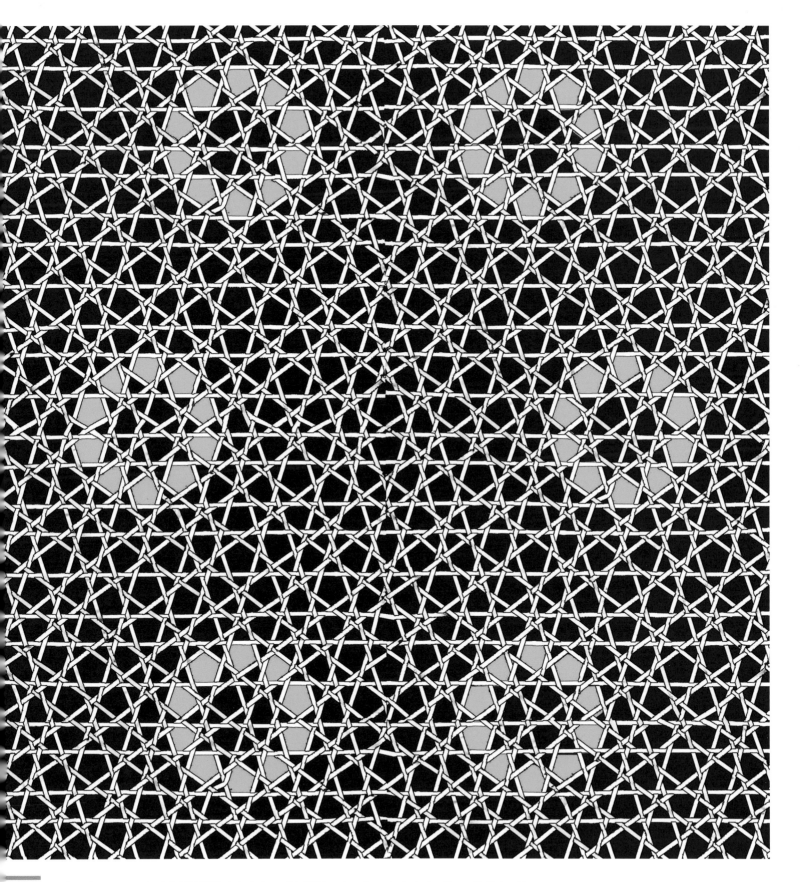

Title: pentagitter [pentagonal grid], 173/178, dated June 24, 2011; artwork and photo by Franz R. Schmid

Gener

02

al
Information

General Informa-tion

Terms and Definitions

As in other areas of textile techniques, there are no generally accepted and common terms and definitions for basketry techniques. Basket weavers in their workshops use different words from the specialist staff in a museum, and the translations from other languages do not help matters much. The following terms and definitions apply to the basketry techniques used in this book. Where it makes sense to me, I have used pictograms to supplement the matters presented.

Thread or Fiber

> Basic material for manufacturing textiles of all kinds
> Flexible, narrow, linear material that makes it possible to create durable connections with itself or with other materials due to its optimal flexibility
> Can be flat, round, oval, or hollow in cross section

Weaving Element

A thread or fiber according to the above definition, which is processed into a woven structure by using basketry technique.

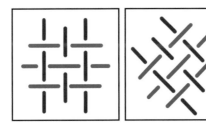

Two examples of structures made of crossed thread or fiber elements.

Thread or Fiber Connections

Threads or fibers can create connections with themselves or with other threads or fibers, when a thread or fiber, or a part thereof, is passed over, under, or through other threads or fibers or parts thereof. The crossing points thus created are responsible for the stability of a structure.

Grain of the Weaving Elements

The grain of the weaving elements (textile grain) signifies the direction in which the individual weaving elements run through the resulting structure during the work process.

There are four possible ways:
> horizontal
> vertical
> diagonal in the S direction
> diagonal in the Z direction

(To make it possible to note the diagonal direction for the weaving elements, we rely on the letters S and Z, which have central lines running from top left to bottom right and from top right to bottom left, respectively.)

Textile Technique

According to the "Basel Nomenclature for Textile Techniques," all processes for the manufacture, processing, and decoration of threads or fibers and fabrics of all kinds belong to the textile techniques, such as spinning, knitting, weaving, cloth weaving, sewing, embroidery, dyeing, etc.

Fabric

The above nomenclature defines fabrics as "two- or three-dimensional products in which individual threads or groups of threads are connected, one to another, by using textile techniques." If applied according to the definition of thread given above, a basket made of willow rods is considered to be just as much a fabric as a piece of the finest silk gauze or a knitted sweater. In this book, I use the terms "structure" and "weave" as synonymous with fabric and in general mean a structure, a construction of individual elements.

Weave or Basketwork

A completely handmade, durable two- or three-dimensional structure of more or less straight-running thread or fiber elements of limited length. In this structure, the threads or fibers intersect according to set rules or can also completely freestyle. During the weaving process, the direction in which elements run may also change, for example, when turning then along a side edge.

Straight Line

By this I mean that the thread does not form loops, as in a knitted fabric, which are connected one to the other, but rather the individual threads continue to run more or less without curving, even after crossing other threads.

Weaving

The work process necessary to make a weave. In weaving, a certain number of weaving elements are manipulated so that they are alternately passed over each other or through each other and thereby form a durable structure.

In contrast to the definition of "weaving" given above, for the specialized area of weaving cloth:

Woven Cloth

A durable, two-dimensional structure of (almost) any length, made of linearly running thread or fiber elements, manufactured with the aid of devices and aids. In this process, the threads intersect lengthwise and crosswise according to specified patterns. During the work process, a portion of the threads are always fixed as a so-called warp, and shedding is done mechanically.

Ready-Made Caning for Chair Seats and Decorations

Looms can also use stiff strips to weave, and the fabrics manufactured in this way are used to make chair seats and garden furniture. Diagonals can be additionally woven into such a basic fabric by hand, for example, to make the yard goods used for the so-called Thonet or Vienna coffee house chairs.

Weaving Pattern

Also called weaving rhythm, weaving step, or form of binding. This refers to repetitive, countable weaving movements, often specified by numbers, such as over 2/under 2, 2/2, 1/1, and so forth. Many weaving patterns have names that are also commonly used for weaving cloth, for example, linen or plain weave, twill weave, atlas, Panama, and houndstooth.

Shedding

To simplify the work processes, you can count off threads running in one direction in a certain sequence and temporarily raise them to make room for a thread running in the other direction (see page 66). In basket weaving, such counting off is done entirely by hand, while in cloth weaving it is done on the loom, using so-called heddles and treadles.

Working Line / Working Edge

This is the borderline between the unwoven threads and the finished fabric. The working line or working edge is, so to speak, where the event happens—here is where the actual work is being done in a specific manner, right now.

For basket weaving, a working line can be horizontal, vertical, diagonal, or circular:

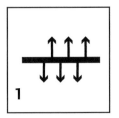

1. Horizontal working edge in orthogonally woven structures

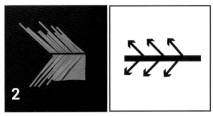

2. Cross-grain, horizontal working edge for diagonally woven structures

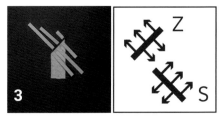

3. With the grain, Z- or S-shaped working edge for diagonally woven structures

4. V-shaped working edge for diagonally woven structures

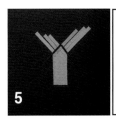  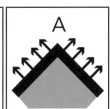

5. A-shaped working edge for diagonally woven structures

  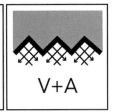

6. Zigzag working edge on diagonally woven structures, a combination of A- and V-shaped working edges

7. O-shaped/circular working edge for cross-grain orthogonally or diagonally woven structures

The names of the individual weaving techniques vary likewise. To me, the most accurate method seems to be by observing in how many directions the woven elements are running and by observing how the weaving elements involved in the structure are interwoven with each other.

There are four main ways:

01. orthogonally in two directions
02. diagonally in two directions
03. in more than two directions
04. by twining

Orthogonally Woven, Orthogonal Weave

Definition of "orthogonal"

I use the word "orthogonal" to designate situations in which the weaving elements are horizontal and perpendicular to each other in space.

› In relation to an imaginary lengthwise axis through the finished product, the weaving elements run horizontally, vertically, or orthogonally through the structure.
› During the weaving process, the weaving elements intersect at right angles.
› While constructing the structure, you must add weaving elements consecutively.
› The working edges are horizontal or vertical.
› Orthogonally woven structures are distinctly elastic along the diagonal.

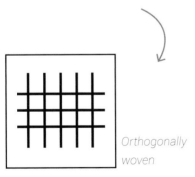

Orthogonally woven

Diagonally Woven, Diagonal Weave

› In relation to an imaginary lengthwise axis through the finished product, the weaving elements run through the structure in two diagonal directions.
› Elements can intersect at right angles or at more obtuse or more acute angles.
› Typical of this type of weave is the amazing fact that after starting the piece of basketwork, no new material at all is added (except for increasing/decreasing). The surfaces or entire shapes are constructed exclusively by using the weaving elements that are already there.
› The working edges can be cross-grain, in the S direction, in the Z direction, A shape, V shape, or zigzag.
› Diagonally woven structures are distinctly elastic lengthwise and crosswise.
› Depending on the work method, striking, clearly visible curved lines are created between the tighter and looser areas in the weave—due to the cramming-spacing effect.

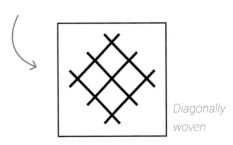

Diagonally woven

The Cramming-Spacing Effect

Noémi Speiser first described this phenomenon, using the name "cramming-spacing." Diagonally woven structures sometimes display curved lines that the weaver did not weave intentionally to create a special pattern, but can be explained only by the work method chosen. In general, the elements that were raised as a group for the shedding step tend to cram together, while the individual elements inserted in the respective shed tend to lie stretched farther apart. If the person doing the weaving is working along a diagonal or zigzag working edge, the weaving elements then change their S and Z directions in phases, so that sometimes one element is more tightly crammed, sometimes the others. This explains the more or less distinct curved lines. The effect is most pronounced when weaving in plain weave (over 1/under 1). With a cross-grain working line, on the other hand, there is always an even balance between the S and Z directions since the weaving elements move over only a very short distance.

Weaving in Several Directions, Multidirectional Weave

› Here, more than two directions come into play for the weaving elements. That is why we also speak of multidirectional weaving.
› Three directions: two diagonals plus one horizontal
› Four directions: two diagonals plus one vertical plus one horizontal; for example, the seat of a Vienna coffee house chair

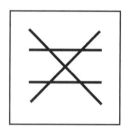

Woven in three directions

Woven in four directions

Impact of the cramming-spacing effect (1/1 diagonally woven), detail of a mat, pandanus, Vanuatu

Impact of the cramming-spacing effect (multicolored, 1/1 diagonally woven)

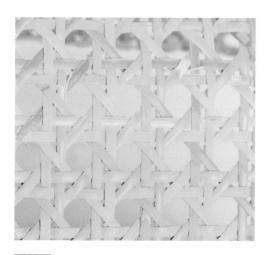

Detail of the canework for a Vienna coffee house chair, rattan chair caning

Twining Weave

Some special conditions apply for this extensive category within basket-weaving techniques:

› The weaving elements do not act as single fibers, but always in groups of two or in teams of several parallel fibers.
› These pairs or teams pass through other previously assembled warp fibers. Between each pair of lengthwise warp fibers, the pairs also intersect each other once again.
› Thus, this does not fulfill the feature required in the definition on page 35 (weaving elements running straight through the structure).

Due to this complexity and the fact that strips are comparatively rarely used as weaving material, I have excluded twining techniques from this book. We will encounter this technique only as a possible method to temporarily secure a structure.

Ready-woven objects can be divided into the following product groups:

1 Plait* or woven braid trim

A braid trim is a long, band-like, narrow weave of strips of material; when made of straw, they are called a straw plait. A braid trim can in theory be of any length.

2 Mat

A mat is a larger two-dimensional weave (rectangular, oval, round) made of strips of material. The mat can (but does not have to) expand on all four sides; that is, at least in theory, a mat can be of any size wanted.

3 Basket

A basket is a three-dimensional woven artifact, open on one side. It can be of any size and shape; there are hardly any limits.

4 Tube

A tube is a cylindrical woven piece that expands along a circular working edge. A tube can also be a specific kind of cylinder with a closed, linear starting piece and a circular upper opening.

5 Enclosed objects

Enclosed objects can be woven loosely or tightly (see the balls on pages 24 and 174). If a weave is woven over a form that remains in the woven piece (see the carrying ring on page 115), you could speak of an "encircling weave."

* The term "plait" is mostly used if the materials or strands of material used have a round cross section.

Different kinds of braid trims made using streamers / carnival streamers

Ibu Nani cuts pandanus leaves for a mat into strips, Krayan, Long Rungan, North Kalimantan, Indonesia.
Photo: Margrit Linder

Strips, homemade or bought ready made

Materials

GENERAL REMARKS

The materials that can be used for weaving are countless—you can consider using anything and everything that is reasonably long and flexible; that is, fiber-like. Some materials grow in such a way that they are immediately "ready for weaving," while others can be bought ready-made, and others have to be prepared with more or less care.

Plastic and corrugated iron have supplanted many traditional materials. Today, for example, "palm leaf tiles" are not used as frequently to cover roofs as was done in the past, and woven baskets are used less often than they were before the introduction of standardized plastic containers. It is interesting that many basket substitute products still mimic the image of basketwork made of natural materials—as if people simply do not want to do without their baskets! Plastic bands and strips work well for weaving.

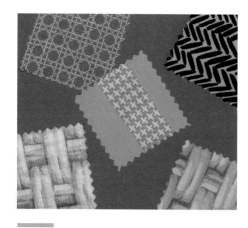

Weaving as a design for printed fabric

Storage basket made of plastic industrial injection molding

Baskets made of plastic.
Staffan Scherz, Wikimedia Commons CC-SA-2.0

Coexistence of traditional materials and plastic, Vietnam.
Photo: Christine Zbinden

The material, which starts out wide, is cut into narrower strips.

Creating the impression of a strip by placing two elements side by side

PREPARING PLANT MATERIALS

You can work with plant materials that are either freshly cut or dried. Please note the following:

› Freshly interwoven material shrinks after it dries.
› Dried bark, straw, flat rattan reed, pond plants, and similar materials must be softened by moistening or soaking before they are used for weaving. Keep the material damp during the weaving process (with a damp sponge or spray bottle).
› Tear leaves of plants into strips by using your fingernail or a pin.
› Flatten and smooth grass stalks; split straw stalks.
› Several narrow elements placed side by side can work like one strip.
› Strips can also be cut into narrower elements during the weaving process.

Dividing a leaf of the Ñocha plant (Eryngium paniculatum) into strips, Ñocha painting, artisans, Chile

Dried willow bark, peeled by hand

Fresh leaves of Phormium tenax (New Zealand flax)

PREPARING PAPER

Strips of paper make a wonderful material for weaving. There are several ways to prepare paper so it can be used for weaving:

Fold strips over four times.

Paper that is too light or printed on one side can be folded. If folded over four times, all the sharp edges have been eliminated; the paper has a good feel and is easy to weave.

› First step: Fold the strips lengthwise.
› Second step: Open the strip again and smooth it out.
› Third step: Fold both lengthwise halves from the outside against the center line and at the same time maintain a distance of about 1–2 mm (0.4–0.8 inches) to the center.
› Fourth step: Place the folded halves one upon the other.
› These strips can be telescoped into each other to make them longer.

Other ways to prepare paper

› Before cutting, stiffen the paper using paste, white glue, acrylic paint, or other adhesives.
› Woven cloth can stiffened in the same way.
› The backs of posters, maps, and so on can be enhanced by applying a collage of paste and colored magazine paper. Iron after drying (while placing silk or baking parchment under the iron).
› Decorate the strips before weaving with them (using seams, writing, patterns, etc.).
› Color, paint, or print the paper sheets yourself.
› Make your own paper and cut or tear it into strips.

Fold paper over four times.

Woven strips of maps folded over four times

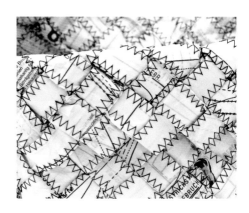

Collage of paste and magazine paper

Paper, folded and sewn

Fiber-like paper yarn

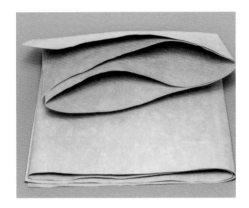

Vegan leather, washed and ironed

Paper galore

Ready-Made Strip Materials

› paper strips for quilling and making folded stars
› paper tape (from the paper yarn trade)
› gift-wrapping ribbon
› raffia viscose
› woodchip, veneer strips
› rattan cane, flat rattan reed, willow splints, etc.
› saleen wicker (synthetic, waterproof, long-lasting wicker)
› plastic packaging tape
› strips of leather
› ready-made straw plaits
› strands, flat wires, metal bands

A roll of saleen (artificial wicker made in Germany)

MATERIALS THAT WORK WELL FOR CUTTING INTO STRIPS

› paper of all kinds, in a whole sheet or from a block: drawing paper, Ingres paper, toned drawing paper, thin paper board, sketching paper, packing paper, tracing paper, glossy paper, elephant hide paper, bamboo paper, map paper, tapa, etc.
› wallpaper from the roll or pattern books
› felt, fleece fabrics
› truck tarpaulins, awning cloth, canvas, Tyvek
› coated fabrics
› foils of all kinds
› leather-look paper (vegan leather)
› leather, imitation leather

SOURCING MATERIALS

To buy or to collect? Usable materials are often lying around unnoticed as waste, such as wastepaper, maps, posters, electric cables, packaging tape, cover sheeting, and long leaves from the garden or pond. There is a huge range of offerings available in handicraft shops, home improvement stores, and hobby markets and flea markets, and of course, there are materials for making strips available ready-made and ready to order on the internet.

Note: You will find relevant sources of supply in the appendix on page 197.

Cross Section

We basically distinguish between weaving materials with a flat or a round cross section. Not all the material cross sections work well for every weaving technique and vice versa. In the practical part of this book, we will be working with stiff materials with a flat cross section—here called a "strip" or "band." The cross section may change; for example, a fresh, flat leaf may curl up as it dries out.

Definition of "Strips"

Flat, rather stiff, but quite flexible fiber of a certain width and limited length; for example, a strip of paper from a DIN A4 sheet

Definition of "Band" or "Tape"

Flat, rather stiff, but quite flexible fiber of a certain width and of (almost) any length, such as gift-wrapping ribbon on a roll

Definition of "Splint"

Splints are a special form of strips. Splints are made by splitting a piece of material with a round cross section lengthwise into several pieces and then planing or smoothing the pieces flat on the underside. Splints have a slightly arched top side. Examples: rattan splints, willow splints, hazel splints, etc.

Visual Impact of the Material

› Sometimes (for example, when shaping a selvage edge), the top or bottom of the strip of material will be reversed during the work process. For example: paper with different colored front and back sides changes color when it is turned over the side edge.

› For many plants, the top of the leaf is shinier and smoother than the bottom.

› Certain material processing methods (see above) determine the appearance of the material; see, for example, the arched top of splints, or the effect of folding paper four times.

› If the strips are not really stiff (such as strips of cloth), they can become very bunched up and creased as you work with them. Results: these weaving elements are no longer clearly recognizable as flat strips, although they move like strips.

Tools and Aids

TOOLS

Our ten fingers are the most important tool for weaving the actual basketwork. Both hands are used equally. At any one point, one hand is working primarily doing the weaving, and the other hand is holding the material fast; then it's the other way around. Many techniques are worked "in space," so to speak, and, at most, just require scissors to shorten any strip ends that are too long.

If the material isn't already shaped in a strip, you will need tools to cut the strips. The second most important tool is therefore a cutting tool: a pair of scissors, a knife, or a paper cutter. Important with any cutting tool: take care when using it. Note that paper cut with a knife may have sharp edges.

AIDS

Flat Underlay

This can be a table or an ironing board, but also the floor, which works especially well, particularly when making large-sized woven pieces.

Basting Thread

A piece of simple household string or the remnant of some thread can be used as basting thread for some work, such as if there is a risk that a woven surface will come apart or shift too soon. Once the basting thread has done its job, it is either removed again or left as a decoration.

Clothespins

Small clothespins from the craft shop (or from the children's room) are worth their weight in gold if you have to temporarily secure your work from coming apart or if you simply need a third hand.

Our ten fingers are the most important tool for weaving basketwork.

The floor as an ideal workplace; here, strips folded over four times in the background

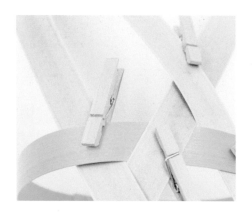

Clothespins used as an aid

Painter's Masking Tape

This adhesive tape helps to temporarily secure weaving elements. If you do not press it down too hard, it can be removed easily and without leaving any residue.

Double-Sided Transparent Tape

This is ideal to invisibly lengthen paper strips.

Sticky Notes

Sticky notes work well to group weaving elements together. The starting ends of the weaving elements, temporarily fastened together, can later be easily detached from the sticky note paper and woven back into the finished weave.

Glue

I do not like using glue to make the weaving elements longer, because the connections become rigid when they dry. It is okay to use glue if you do so selectively; for example, when securing the strip ends (by working the ends back into the finished weave). Just put a blob of it on a piece of paper and apply with a toothpick.

Pins

Pins and a pad suitable for using the pins are especially helpful when starting a piece of basketwork; for example, to create a starting line.

Forms

If you want to achieve a specific shape, you can use a solid form, such as a can or box. The form should not be narrower at the top than at the bottom; otherwise you cannot take it off.

Weights and Clamping Devices

Sometimes, it is practical to have the resulting piece of basketwork under slight tension. This can be achieved by weighing it down using a weight (your own foot, a stone, a filled bottle, a full can, etc.).

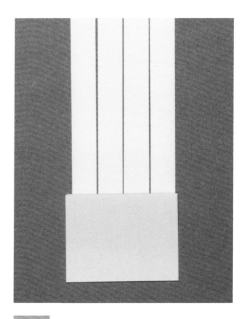

Four strips of paper in a "sandwich" between two sticky notes.

Weighing down the work using your own foot, twill pattern, orthogonally woven from purun/sedge (Lepironia articulata), Sempayang, North Kalimantan, Indonesia. Photo: Margrit Linder

Working the Materials

Turning Over

This refers to folding over a whole piece of work or a woven strip—just like leafing through a book. When you do this, what used to be the back becomes the new front.

Turning/Rotating

The piece is turned or rotated on the work surface, without reversing the front and back. The rotation can be to the left or right, clockwise or counterclockwise.

Folding

Folding a strip reinforces and stabilizes the turning maneuver by applying firm pinching/creasing. For example, with a strip of paper, the folded part is presented with its backside facing upward; the trace of folding remains permanently visible.

With one strip, you basically have only two possible ways to move it:

01. Fold it over forward
02. Fold it over backward

<u>Note</u>: In the figure, the folds are shown at a slight angle to make it clearer. In practice, you fold the strips in such a way that they either lie directly atop each other or at right angles to each other.

If you only turn the strip without creasing it, the result is a loose loop that is only temporary, used to make certain knots.

Strips in loop form, strips folded over front to back

Lengthening strips of weaving elements

Typically, it becomes necessary to keep lengthening the materials, which are of limited length, during the weaving process. Exceptions: small-scale work, using yard goods.

Possible Ways to Lengthen:
› Lengthen by overlapping: Work with doubled strips for a few centimeters, then keep on weaving with only the new element. Leave the ends alone or cut them off. [1]
› Lengthen the strip by fastening the new material, using glue, adhesive film (possibly visible), or double-sided adhesive tape (not visible). [2]
› Lengthen the strip, using staples. [2]
› Lengthen the strip, using slot connectors. [3]

Growth Direction of the Finished Weave

A weave grows along the working line. Imagining the direction of growth is a somewhat abstract process; it is easier to observe where the finished weave is moving: away from you or toward you?

When you are reading the instructions in this book, if you should ever feel that you would rather weave the other way around (such as an A-shaped working edge instead of a V-shaped one), try it out! You often have the freedom to choose between different ways of working, without being able to see these as of yet in the finished weave. Take a piece of knitting for comparison: the finished knit fabric definitely grows toward you and falls into your lap—you do not have the option of knitting the other way round.

Starting a Piece of Basketwork

There are many different ways to start a piece of basketwork. Beginning on page 68, you will learn about them and the associated pictograms.

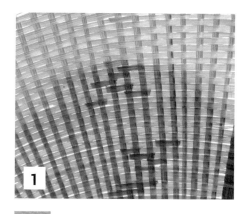

Lengthening by overlapping against backlight: fans from India

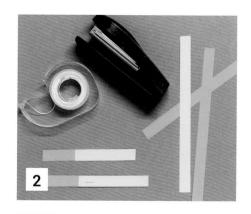

Aids for lengthening

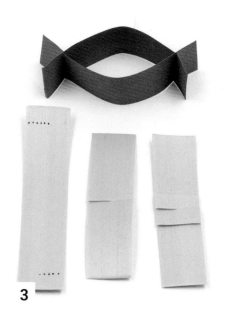

Lengthening using slot connectors: double slot connector (top), simple slot connector (below), position of the cuts (bottom left), front and back of the slot connector (middle and bottom right)

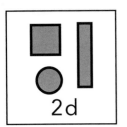

Constructing bands and surfaces

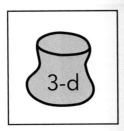

Three-dimensional artifact

Constructing Bands, Surfaces, and Artifacts

As you will see in the chapters on the groups of techniques, there are all sorts of different ways to construct bands, surfaces, and artifacts.

Edges

Weaving the edges or rims on basketwork pieces is often a special challenge: starting edges, selvages, finished edges. You usually have several options that must be carefully calibrated to the type of finished weave. How should the edges or rims look—smooth, zigzag or serrated, fringed or simply cut off? We can also call finished edges selvages, and we speak, for example, of side selvages (details about the edges or rims are explained in the respective technical chapters).

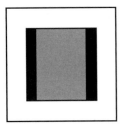

Freestyle rim

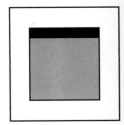

Sewn finished edge

Increasing or Decreasing the Number of Weaving Elements

Increasing and decreasing the number of weaving elements opens up a wide range of possibilities for shaping the work. You can insert extra elements into the structure or combine elements and work with them like single elements. As you do so, it is necessary to find a solution appropriate for the materials. In many hats or placemats, increasing or decreasing the weaving elements is often masterful work.

Straight side edges

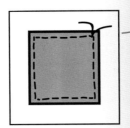

Straight finished edge

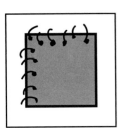

Finished edge with extra elements

Adding weaving elements at the center of the circle; place mat of paper yarn

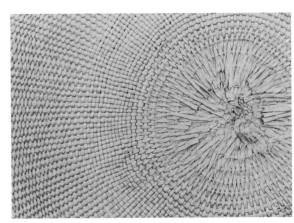

Serrated side edges

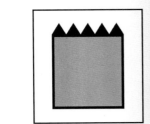

Serrated finished edge

Introducing a new weaving element, saleen wicker

A whole lot of ends to work back into the weave, rattan basket, diagonally woven, 15 x 15 x 15 cm, Agabag people, Tanjung Harapan, North Kalimantan, Indonesia. Photo: Margrit Linder

Weaving elements worked back into the inside of the basket.

Weaving elements worked into the outside of the basket

Finishing a Piece of Basketwork

Again, there are different ways to finish a piece of basketwork:

> Fold over the as-yet-unwoven weaving element ends to the outside (or inside, but this is more laborious) and work them back into the finished weave. This makes the rim areas of the structure double-sided, and thus thicker and stronger.
> Secure the finished weave with staples, with glue, by sewing, or other means.
> Cut off the ends of the weaving elements.
> Leave the ends of the weaving elements as a fringe.
> Cover the ends of the weaving elements with extra elements and secure with sewing stitches.

In Switzerland, we use the German word *verstäten*. For sewing, it is used in the sense of stitching up or neatening the thread ends. I will use it in this book as a term for securing excess basketwork ends.

Definition of *Verstäten*:
Working the basketwork ends back into the finished weave.

Trim the Ends
> Before trimming, pull a little on the element end and then cut it off. This causes the worked-in element to be drawn back into the weave.
> Instead of cutting them off, trim the ends into fringes.
> If the elements are still long enough, leave them extended as "curls" (see page 188).

Perfect interplay of material and technique: pliant fall of a basket-weave bag

Creative Potential

In my view, there is an enormous potential for creativity in all weaving techniques. In addition to the criteria of function, construction, and proportion, there may be other interesting factors, which I would like to introduce below.

DIMENSIONS

Unlike using a loom, basket weaving allows you to be free to expand as far as you want in any dimension. There are techniques that are better for long, narrow weaves and techniques that are a good choice for short, wide weaves. It is important to consider what is best for the idea of the product being made.

THE CHARACTER OF THE STRUCTURE

Tightness

In many techniques, it is possible to weave strips of material both tightly and like a sieve (open or light weave).

Structure Properties Related to Technique

Many interesting properties of the finished structures are related to the technique used. For example, if it is necessary for a finished weave to have elasticity, this will depend on whether the structure is woven orthogonally, diagonally, or in several directions. You should take note of the following:

› Orthogonally woven structures are elastic along the diagonal.
› Diagonally woven structures are elastic lengthwise and crosswise.
› Structures woven in several directions are (almost) non-elastic.

Selection of Materials

In addition to the technique, the materials that the weaver selects significantly influence the character of the woven structure (wavy, pliable, flowing, or stiff).

Forming the pattern during the
weaving process (detail), rattan bag,
diagonally woven

Openwork pattern on a hat

PATTERNS AND DECORATIONS

Patterns are either formed already during the weaving process or subsequently applied to the finished structure.

"Weaving a raised pattern" in a 1/1 diagonally woven bamboo structure (detail)

HANGING OR SETTING UP

› The typical small holes in a weave of strips let you use nails or pins to hang up a piece. If you fasten several nails into the width, even large weaves can be easily hung on the wall without using an extra rod.

› Extra rods, which can be hung on nails, for example, can easily be pulled through a finished weave of strips.

› Long weaves can be rolled up and set up, which lets you create interesting arrangements in a room.

Mat made of map paper, hung up on a nail, 1/1 orthogonally woven

Mat made of map paper, rolled and set up, 1/1 orthogonally woven

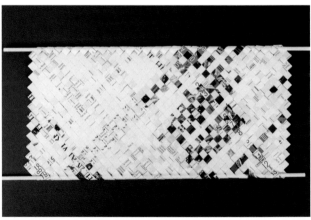

Mat with inserted rods, 1/1 diagonally woven, calendar paper

REINFORCING

There are various ways to reinforce or stiffen a piece of basketwork:

› Add extra strips, struts, or supports to the edges or rims of the piece; these can sometimes also be decorative.
› Stiffen the finished woven product (with paint, resin, or glue).

Rod woven into a basket to make a foot, North Kalimantan, Indonesia

Reinforcing and decorative elements, woven in and applied, on a diagonally woven basket from North Kalimantan, Indonesia

Basket bowl with painted extra strips and inner rim reinforcement, twill pattern. Origin: Mozambique, Limpopo plain; materials: grass stalks, wooden sticks, woodchip, grass cord, paint; diameter: 21.5 cm, height: 11 cm. Ethnographic Museum at the Univeristy of Zurich,, Inventory No. 08613a/b. Photo: Kathrin Leuenberger

Support elements on a basket base, 1/1 diagonally woven, bamboo, Laos

Detail of inserted basket handle

Inserted cord as a handle solution

Detail of woven-in handle

CARRYING DEVICES

Many weaves are used for carrying and require appropriate devices to do this. These can be inserted into the finished weave afterward or woven in directly.

Attached handle solution

Detail of a woven-in strap

ADDING

Adding and sequencing are methods that invite experimentation. The principle of building something large from smaller individual parts is applied in many handcrafted products—be it a patchwork quilt, a necklace made of glass beads, or other items.

Individual conical elements added to a wreath (see page 138), music note paper, 1/1 orthogonally woven

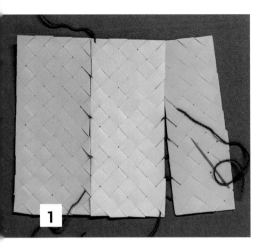

Sewing pieces of braid trim together with thread

Sewing Items Together

A special method of adding is to sew together narrow pieces of braid trim and plait to surfaces and artifacts. Classic examples of these are straw hats and beach bags. How to proceed:

› Sew the overlapping side edges of the braid trim together by machine (figures 3 and 4).
› Then sew the side edges of the braid trim together by hand, following the weaving pattern (figures 1, 2, and 5).
› Weave them to each other directly, following the weave pattern (see page 111).

Pieces of braid trim stitched together to form a bag (detail), twill, 2/2 diagonally woven, palm leaf, Kenya

Case made by sewing palm leaf braid trim together, various woven patterns, Bahamas

Experiment: Use the sewing machine to sew straw plaits together.
Photo: Anna Sonderegger

Child's room carpet, plait made of strips of jersey sewn together

GATHER, COMPRESS, FOLD, ROLL UP

If you choose the appropriate material (pliant, very flexible, tear-resistant, fine), a woven surface can be gathered, rolled, compressed, or folded into any new shape. In doing this, handle the basketwork like a woven piece of cloth.

Purse ("Kotoku"); origin: Ghana, Accra; material: bast; height: 13.3 cm, width: 15 cm, depth: 15.5 cm. Ethnographic Museum at the Univeristy of Zurich, Inventory No. 00104. Photo: Kathrin Leuenberger

Rolled napkin. Origin: Madagascar; material: papyrus; length: 39.8 cm, width: 39.7 cm. Ethnographic Museum at the Univeristy of Zurich, Inventory No. 00055. Photo: Kathrin Leuenberger

Practice and In-Depth Tasks

Working your way through the instructions is a good way to learn the techniques presented in the next chapters. Besides this, I recommend the following approach to practice weaving with strips:

MAKE MISTAKES

› Do not invest any time in unraveling and trying to fix mistakes. Rather, start anew—repetition brings experience!
› It is often possible to derive new ideas from mistakes and detours. Be sure to take notes, so that a "mistake" can later be repeated in a targeted and profitable manner.

Suggestions for setting tasks

› Get yourself some weaving materials other than those mentioned in the book, and try them out.
› Work with the same materials but use a different technique.
› For example, weave to the left instead of to the right.
› Ask yourself questions: Does the size of the planned products affect how the techniques are handled? Is it possible or necessary to work in miniature or extra-large sizes? What happens when you add together, line up, arrange, staple, sew together, or otherwise handle the products?
› Take up an idea and develop designs.

It is often possible to derive new ideas from mistakes and detours.

Develop and realize a product

Nobody ever just gets an idea for a product overnight. Every designer deals with the following questions:

What requirements should the product meet?
What are my aspirations in terms of sustainability?
What technique do I know that could fulfill these requirements?
Which materials would work well?
Which shapes, colors, patterns, and sizes are the right ones?
Are handles, side reinforcements, and so on necessary?
Which material and technique samples should I create so that I can do a size calculation and then calculate the material requirements from this?
How much time do I expect I will need?
Should I make prototypes or models?
What costs for materials and work do I have to reckon with?
What would a flowchart for realizing the project look like?

Finally, here is a hint from one of the most convincing projects I have recently discovered: the lamps made of PET bottles by the ACdO or Alvaro Catalán de Ocón company. This Spanish company knows not only how to focus on the advantages of weaving, but also how to translate factors such as sustainability, recycling, job creation, fair trade, and cultural exchange into a product that is suitable for everyday use. On www.acdo.es, you will find the background and facts about this impressive project, in which workers weave paja tetera (arrowroot plants) or willows a together with strips of PET to make lamps.

Making PET lamps along with artisans in Chimbarongo, Chile. Photo: © ACdO

Making PET lamps along with Japanese artisans in Kyoto. Photo: Yuya Hoshino

Making PET lamps along with Colombian artisans. Photo: © ACdO

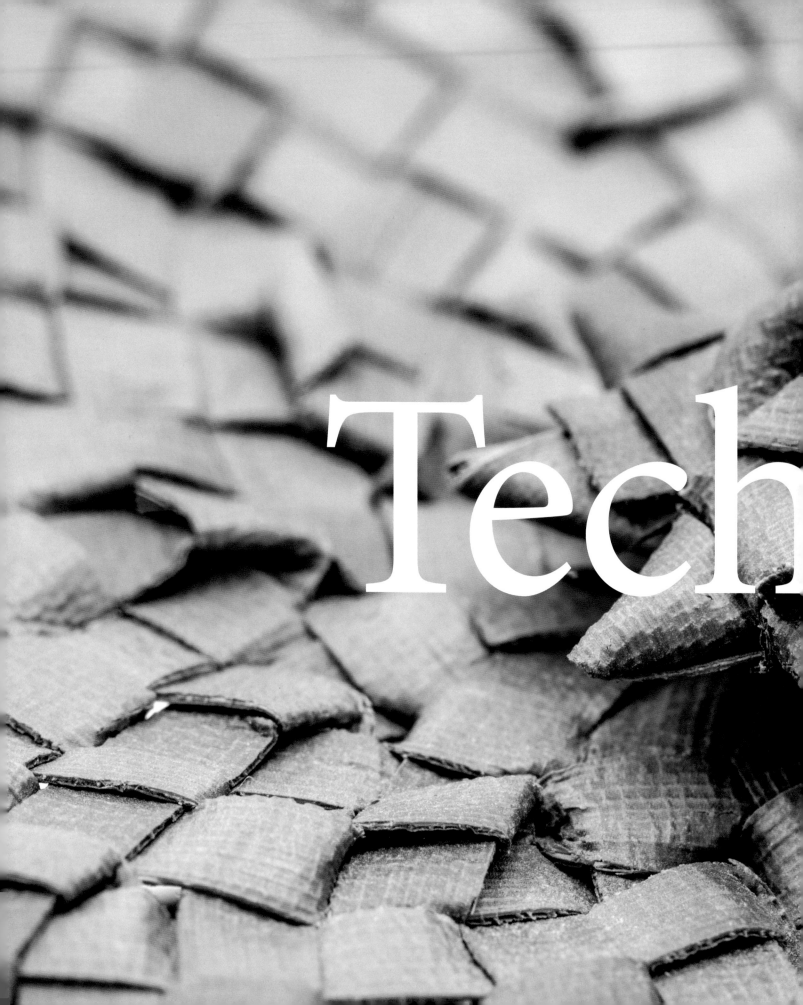

niques

03
Tech-
niques

Introduction to Techniques

I had barely any opportunities to observe other practitioners when I wanted to learn a weaving technique. So I cannot show you how to do it, but just how I have found out over the years that you can actually do this work. In terms of weaving techniques, I am setting the following limitations:

— Limited to exclusively using strip-shaped materials
— Constructing the objects "in one piece" (as opposed to traditional central European baskets, which are made using different techniques for the base, sides, rim, handle, and other parts)
— Subjective selection of projects according to my personal preferences

General Information about This Book

— The instructions will guide you step by step, from the surface to the third dimension.

— Each instruction is also itself a small project at the same time. (Sample pieces look very good on a birthday card, for example!)

— The character of a structure usually emerges only after a few (at least 4–5) rows or rounds—so stick with it!

— You do not need any prior knowledge to get started (technique groups 1 and 2).

— Technique group 3 is based on the principles from technique groups 1 and 2.

— In most cases, it does not matter if the number of weaving elements involved in a structure is even or odd; this is relevant only for certain color effects, symmetries, patterns, or subdivisions of base surfaces—I point out this each time.

Sample workpieces used to decorate a greeting card

Notes on the instructions

Please note that the weaving elements are unnaturally short in the photos for the instructions. This is for the sake of greater clarity. If you are developing a product yourself, you should choose to work with the longest possible weaving elements so you can avoid having to lengthen them too often. The materials I have worked with are listed each time in the instructions, along with other possible alternatives. And, of course, there are many more that would also work well—be inventive and happy to experiment!

There are suggestions for finishing in technique group 2.

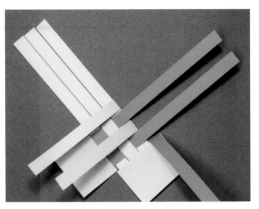 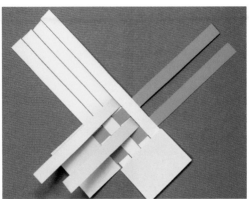 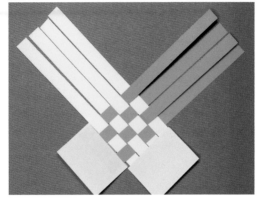

SHEDDING WHEN WEAVING STRIPS

Shedding makes it possible to avoid the annoying slippage of the elements:

› Fold down specific, counted-off elements (you can fold over only an element that is under another one).
› The groups of woven elements formed in this way now point in two directions and form the open shed into which a new element is inserted.
› Then return the folded-over elements to their original position; all weaving elements now point in the same direction and the shed is closed.
› Then open the next shed, and so on.

SECURING THE WEAVE

If the surfaces are to be further worked into three-dimensional objects later, you need to use thread to temporarily secure the weave so that it does not come apart ahead of time (with loose ends on all sides). The weave can be secured by making a round in twining or simple plain weave (over 1/under 1).

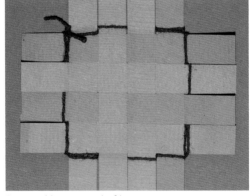 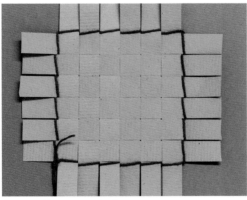

Secured by a round of in plain weave (1/1)

Secured by a round of twining

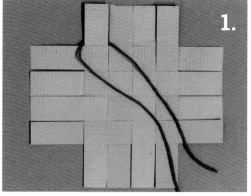

Interlink the thread.

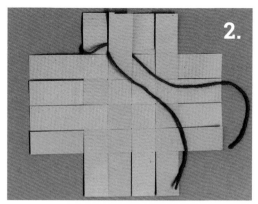

First weaving step

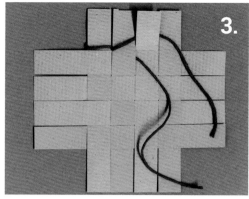

Second weaving step

Instructions for Twining

› Double the thread and interlink it, with the thread ends next to each other. **[1]**

› First weaving step: pass the left thread behind the next weaving element to the front again **[2]**; the threads have been crossed during weaving.

› Second weaving step: again pass the left of the two threads behind a weaving element to the front. **[3]**

› Continue until you have finished the first side. **[4]**

› To weave the second side, turn the piece by 90 degrees, cross the threads in the corner, and continue working. The left of the two thread ends is active while the other waits until it has its own turn. **[5]**

› Continue working in this way, and at the end knot the two thread ends together.

› Align all loose weaving elements to the same length.

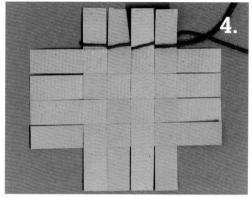

The finished first side

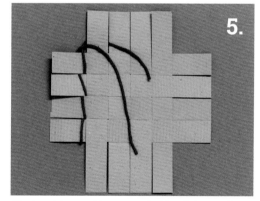

Start twining on the second side of the surface

Technique Group 1

Starting a Project and Constructing a Surface

Working on the starting center for a Panama hat.
Photo: M. M., Sigsig, Ecuador,
Wikimedia Commons CC-SA-2.0

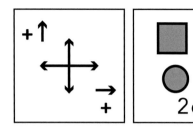

Materials
Strips that can be easily folded, such as paper strips or gift-wrapping ribbon

Note
The front and back sides of the strips in the photos are of different colors, which you can see when they are unfolded.

Variations:
› Insert new elements on only one side.
› Work counterclockwise.
› Use only strips of the same color.
› Use strips of different widths.

Starting from the Center with Loose Weaving Elements and Shedding

Starting from the center works well for making weaves that you want to have loose ends on all sides—for example, as the base for a basket. Besides, if you start out this way, you are still free to decide what the final size of the resulting surface will be.

Starting and constructing the surface—1/1 orthogonally woven.
› Weave four strips of different colors close together orthogonally. **[1 and 2]**
› Fold over the blue strip on the right-hand side. **[3]**
› Insert a new yellow strip parallel to the first yellow strip in the folded over shed. **[4]**
› Unfold the folded-over blue element. **[5]**
› Continue working clockwise on all the other sides, following the same principle. **[6-14]**
› After this round, there will always be two strips of the same color lying next to each other in the growing weave, and the fabric now already has an amazing stability.
› Start a new round of folding and inserting.
› Align all the weaving elements to the same length.

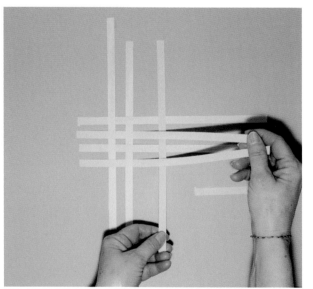

Working with veneer strips: Just lift them up, instead of folding.

WORKING WITH VERY STIFF WEAVING ELEMENTS
Very stiff weaving elements, such as veneer strips, cannot be folded. Instead, lift the strips up slightly and then insert the new element.

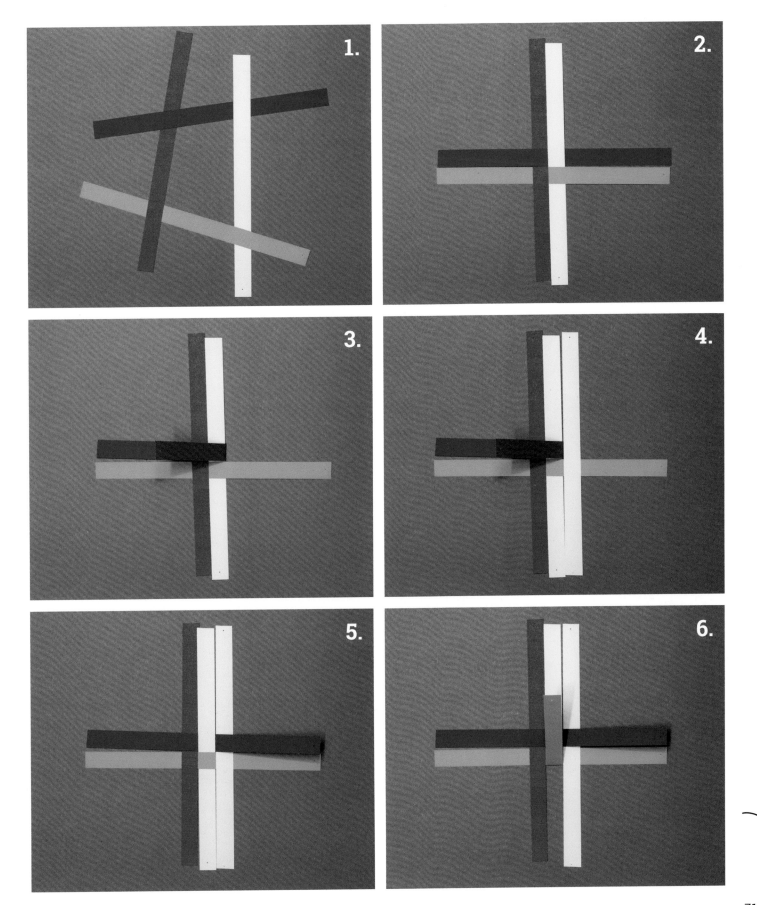

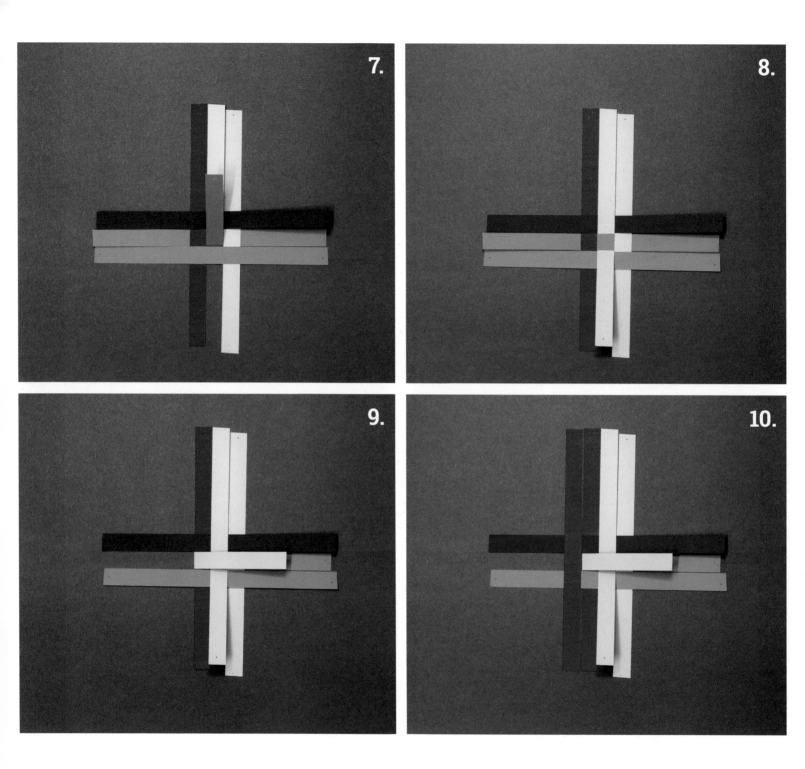

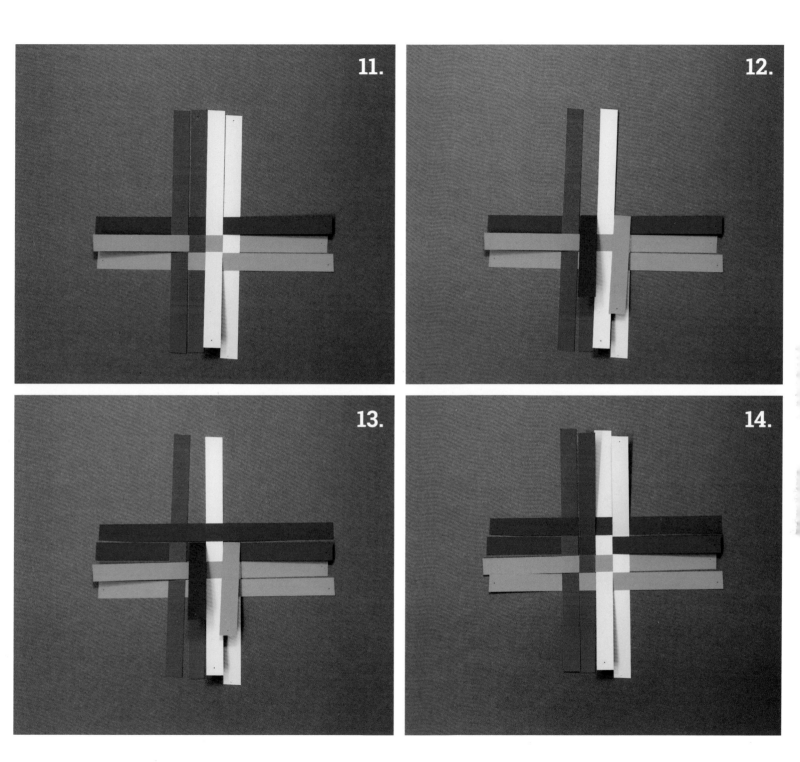

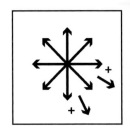

Starting from the Center to Make a Circular Surface

Circular surfaces for making hats, place mats, coasters, carpets, and so forth are made using different ways to start the work from the center:

› Use a small woven bottom piece as a center.
› Use a bundle of woven elements arranged in the shape of a star as a center.
› Use the start of a narrow braid trim (plait) as the center.

The growing radius of the circular surface requires adding extra weaving elements.

Starting from the center in three directions

Starting from the center with plaits

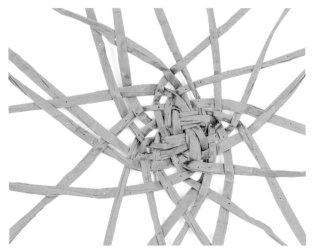

Starting with bundles of weaving elements

Extra weaving elements inserted in a hat (inside)

Circular Surface, Orthogonally Woven

› Starting position: Center with weaving elements one atop the other in radial design. (It is necessary to have an odd number of rays or two staggered weft strands; these must never overtake each other.)
› Weave a single element orthogonally 1/1 into these elements.
› Insert new weaving elements as indicated in the photo.
› If you don't add in any more new elements, the surface will automatically bulge into the third dimension as you continue weaving.

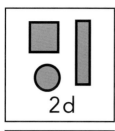
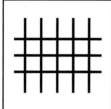
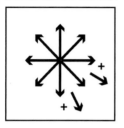

Materials
Paper tape or something similar

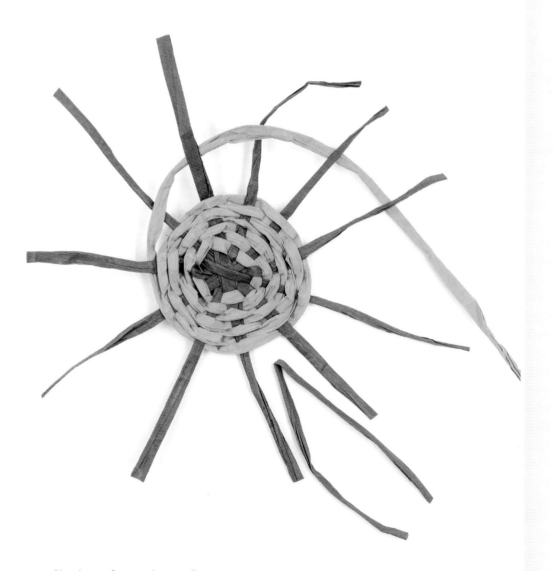

Circular surface, orthogonally woven

Center

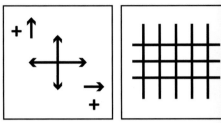

Base

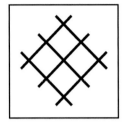 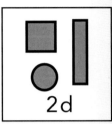

Materials
Paper tape or other pliable strips, such as plant materials or raffia viscose

Aids
Pins and a suitable pad

While working the steps of this project, you can see the intricate craftsmanship and design that goes into the creation of a woven hat!

Circular Surface, Diagonally Woven

> Starting position: Weave a surface of 4 x 4 individual elements (four lengthwise and four crosswise) together orthogonally and not too tightly. **[1]** From now on, the 16 weaving elements act according to the rules of a diagonally woven structure and together form the growing surface. New elements must be inserted as soon as the growing radius makes it necessary.

> **Step 1**: Cross the two central weaving elements on all four working edges **[2]**; secure with pins.

> **Step 2:** Weave the crossed strands together each time 1/1 to the left and right and cross them with the strands of the adjacent working edges **[3]**; arrange the elements in a star shape and secure with pins.

> **Step 3:** Cross the two elements that are directly above the first cross in figure 2 again all around (in the figure, done in Z direction). **[4, right side]**

> **Step 4:** Interlink new elements. **[4, left side]**. (The individual strips are twice as long as necessary and are folded and then linked in.)

> **Step 5:** Now cross the new elements with the ones already there, which takes a lot of work (you need good nerves and lots of pins!). To get a better overview, first arrange the elements so that there are always two of the same color next to each other. **[5, upper section]**

> Continue weaving and adding more elements; while constructing the circular surface, do not leave the (cross-grain) circular working edge. As soon as you stop adding in more new elements, the surface will automatically bulge into the third dimension as you continue weaving. I recommend switching to a V-shaped working edge and continue weaving in sections.

Ibu Tinting weaving a rattan hat, Tanjung Langsat, North Kalimantan, Indonesia.
Photo: Margrit Linder

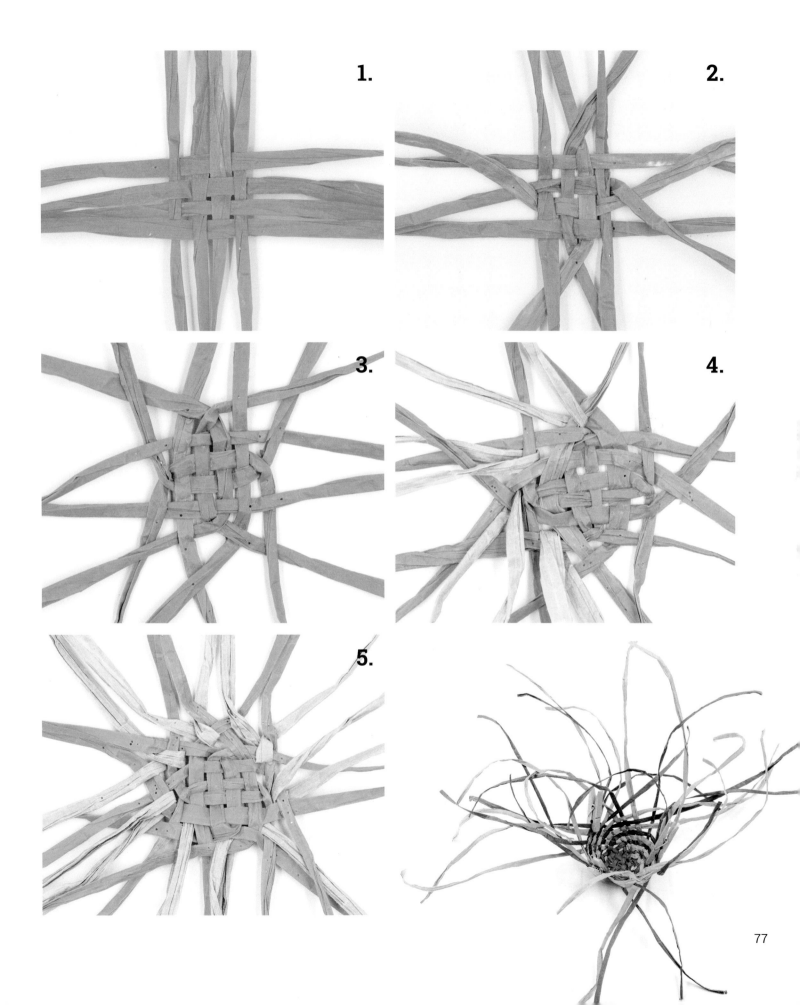

1.

2.

3.

4.

5.

77

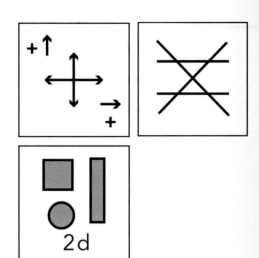

2d

Materials

Stiff strips, such as plastic straps, woodchip, veneer strips, rattan reed, and rattan cane

Tools

A protractor for checking, as needed

Starting from the Center with Loose Weaving Elements Going in Three Directions (Open)

It is extremely difficult to weave a flat piece in three directions in this tightly woven version of this technique. That is why such weaves are sometimes called "mad weaves" in English. An important new angle comes into play here, the 60-degree angle.

Start and construction of the surface, woven 1/1 in three directions

› The material in the photos: paper strips in orange, blue, red
› Arrange the first three elements as shown [1]: The orange strips form the S diagonal (S1) and lie on the red Z diagonal (Z1). The blue horizontal (H1) is above S1 and under Z1. For this first arrangement, stay in approximately the lower third of the area indicated by the diagonal. The point where S1, Z1, and H1 intersect lies under H1 and clearly has the shape of a filled triangle—these triangles are important orientation points!

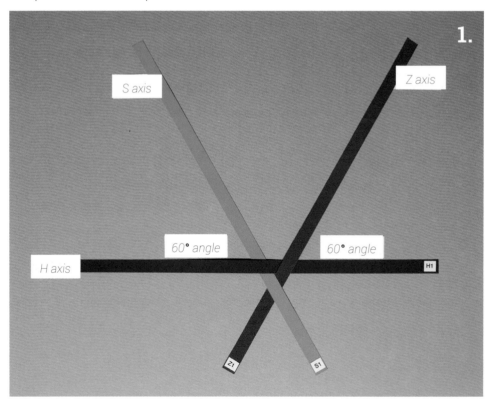

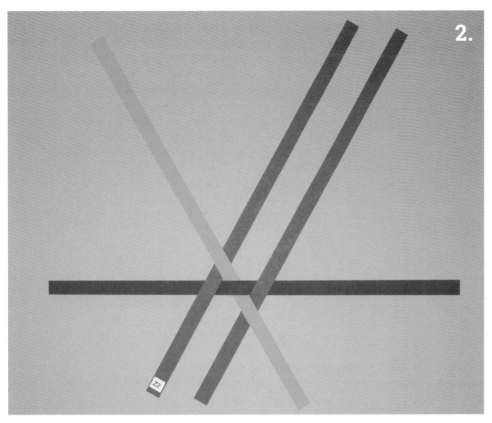

2.

› The second red diagonal Z2 is woven into the left of Z1 and parallel to it. It lies above H1 and under S1—again, this forms a distinct triangle, this time above H1. **[2]**

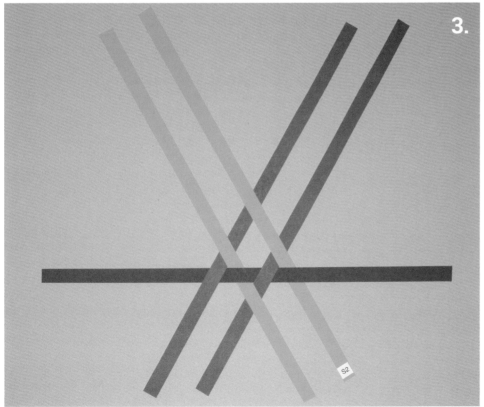

3.

› Weave in S2. S2 lies above the two red diagonals and under H1—a second triangle is formed above H1. **[3]**

› H2 is woven in above H1 and lies under Z1, above S2, under Z2, and above S1—a triangle is formed above H2.
› You can now clearly see a hexagonal hole in the center of all three parallel diagonal pairs. **[4]**

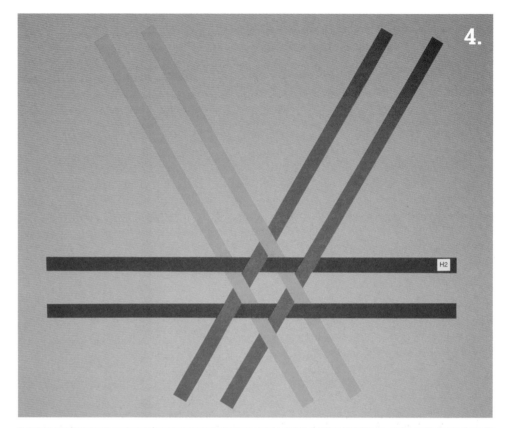

› Continue to weave in new elements in this way, until four elements each of the same color have found their place in every direction in the structure. Orient yourself to the places with tightly woven triangles and hexagonal holes. **[5]**

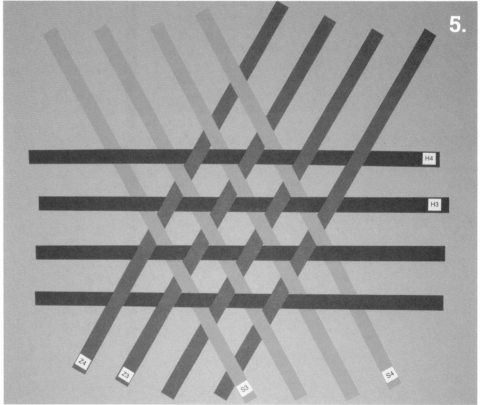

› Align the ends of all weaving elements to the same length. Before pulling on any element to do this, secure it by placing your flat hand in the middle of the finished structure so that none of the angles get twisted.

› A larger hexagon forms the border of the finished structure, and all six side edges have loose elements going in two diagonal directions. **[6]**

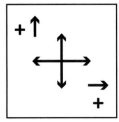

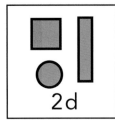

2d

Materials
Stiff, wide strips—made, for example, of drawing paper, plastic straps, wood-chips, veneer strips, etc.

Tools
Pins and a suitable pad

Starting from the Center with Loose Weaving Elements in Four Directions

The woven figure of an Asian rice goddess became the inspiration for the shape of this base. This work is done by expanding the starting point from the center, using four elements. You add another two diagonals going in two directions each time to the two horizontal and vertical elements. This creates a weave in four directions and later a rounded or octagonal base.

If you have cut the weaving elements to be long enough from the start, you can use the base presented here for making the basket shown on page 152.

Start and construction of a flat base, woven 1/1 in four directions

The example in the photos was worked using stiff saleen wicker. How to proceed:

› Tightly weave together two yellow and two white strips 1/1 orthogonally. In figure 1, a red pin highlights the center point. You will see four crossings of white and yellow strips around this center: North of the center point, white lies on yellow (A) at right and yellow on white (B) at left. South of the center point, the situation is exactly the other way around. Yellow lies on white (C) at right, and white lies on yellow (D) at left. **[1]**

› Now weave in the first (right hand) S diagonal (orange) from bottom right to top left. Above the center point, the element passes under the white cross element and under the crossing B; the strip is right against the red pin. Pass the second (left hand) S diagonal (orange) above the center point from the top left, over the crossing B and under the center point, under crossing C; the strip is right up against the red pin. The two orange strips are parallel to each other. **[2]**

› Pass the first (right hand) Z diagonal (beige) under the center point from the bottom left over the white cross element and above the center point, under all the strips lying there, to the top right. Pass the second (left) Z diagonal above the center point from the top right over the white cross element and under the center point, under all elements lying there, to the bottom left. The two beige strips are parallel to each other and complete the image of a star. **[3]**

› Now align all elements to the same length.

› Secure this structure all around with basting thread, using a plain weave (over 1/ under 1). It is not very stable by itself yet. **[4]**

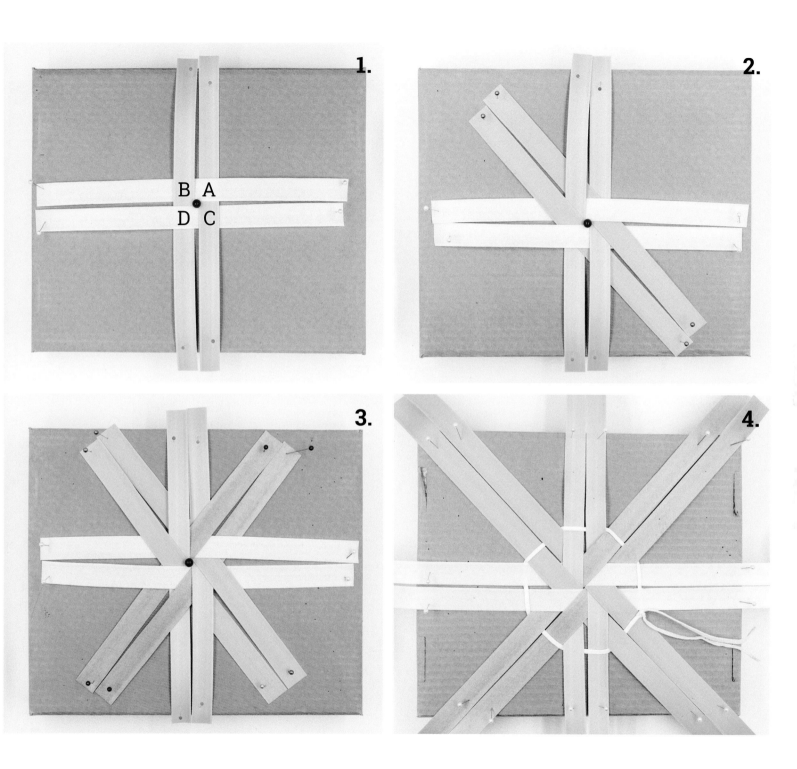

Starting along a Line

There are several ways to start a weave along a straight—usually horizontal—line. Please note that "straight line" refers to the starting situation; the actual working edge (page 36) may be different from the starting line.

Depending on which version of the technique you use, either you create loose weaving element ends along all the edges or the elements are woven in such a way that you already do not leave any loose ends along the starting line and the resulting side edges. Neither version will automatically create a finished edge for any surface; it is necessary to secure the ends of the weaving elements in any case.

Working with Arrowheads

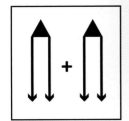

I discovered this clever method in a book about weaving in Hawaii: previously folded elements are woven in in such a way that you create both a finished starting line and secured selvages in a single work step.

In the following, I call this work method "working with arrowheads," since the shape of the folded element reminds me of an arrow.

This method works well with all strip-shaped materials that can be folded without breaking: palm leaves, paper, plastics, gift-wrapping ribbons, and so on. Work as follows:

› Hold one strip horizontally in your hand and fold the right section over backward so that this section of strip forms a right angle to the left section of the strip (the original back side of the right section is facing forward). This creates an edge slanted at a 45-degree angle along the fold. I call the resulting two-section element a "half arrowhead."

› Now make a second fold in this half arrowhead. Fold the left section of the strip in the opposite direction to the first fold; that is, now you fold it over forward. After you have made this fold, the same sides of the strip (the back sides) are facing upward again, except for a small triangular area. The two sections of the strip are parallel to one another and form an "arrowhead" at one end. This has a small triangular slot at the top right, which I will call a "pocket" in the following. This will serve us well later on.

Left: *full arrowhead*; right: *half arrowhead*

More notes about the arrowheads:

› In terms of folding, the front and back sides of these arrowheads are identical.
› It is possible to fold the arrowheads in other ways, such as by working on the same section of the strip and folding it over either to the front or to the back twice in a row.
› The only important thing is that you fold all the arrowheads or half arrowheads you need in the same way.
› In the photo, the ends of the individual weaving elements are about the same length. In practice, however, for example, when making braid trims and flat surfaces, these ends should be of unequal length so that if it is necessary to make the weaving elements longer, you do not have to do this for all of them at the same place in the weave.
› You will automatically always have an even number of weaving elements.

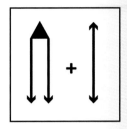

Materials

Paper strips, gift-wrapping ribbon, plant materials, etc.

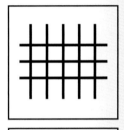

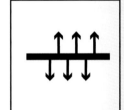

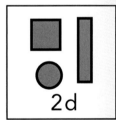

Construction of a braid trim or mat made of arrowheads plus a continuous weft element, orthogonally woven 1/1 along a horizontal working edge

The following steps explain how to start a braid trim using with two arrowheads:

› Make two arrowheads (with ends of irregular length) and place them side by side in such a way that the tips of the arrows point away from you and the pockets lie to the right on the arrows. [1]

› Directly underneath the pockets, fold the strips upward and thus open up a shed. The ends now point in opposite directions, and at the same time, the two right arrowhead elements point away from you. [2]

› Insert the weft element crosswise in the open shed. [3]

› Close the shed and open a new one; this will already hold the weft strip really fast. Pull the weft element to the left, except for a small remnant (which stays still), and fold the strip over forward. [4] Important: only two strips are lying alongside the arrowheads; three strips are pointing toward you.

› Now fold the weft strip over again and put it in the open shed to the right. This forms a point, just like those on the arrowheads, on the side edge of the resulting braid trim. [5]

› Close the shed. [6]

› Open a new shed. [7] Fold the weft strip over twice forward and put it in the open shed. [8–9]

› Continue to work in this way. To make a braid trim, you have to keep lengthening both of the arrowhead elements as well as the weft element; for example, by overlapping or gluing on new elements. This creates serrated selvages on the braid trim. [10]

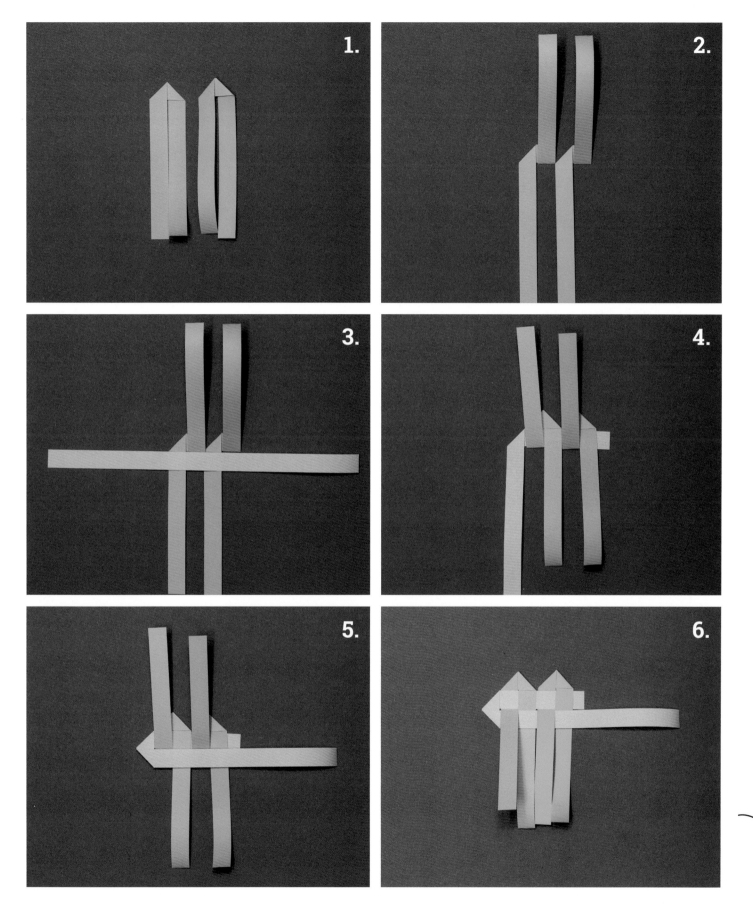

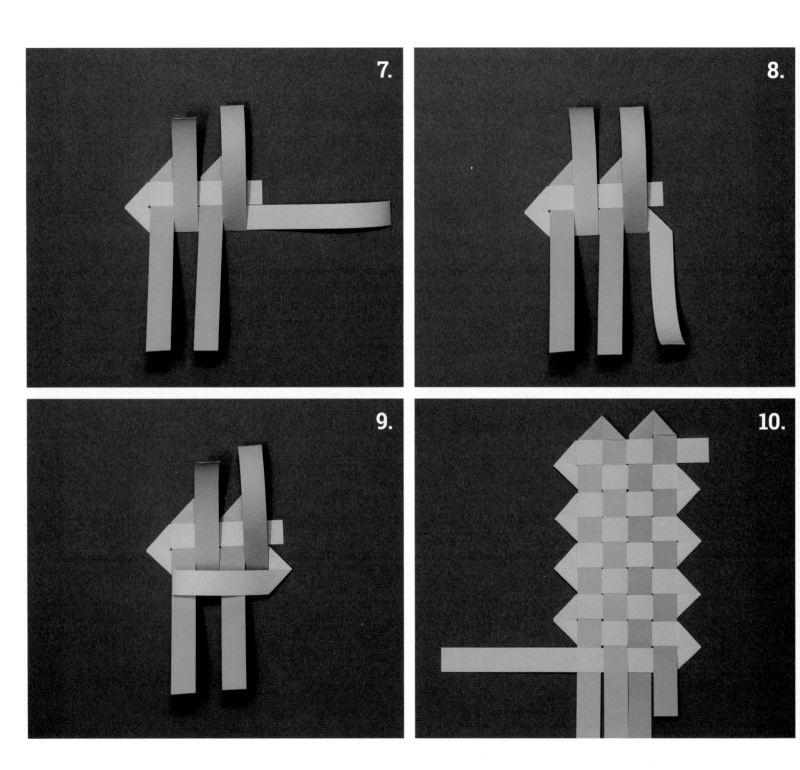

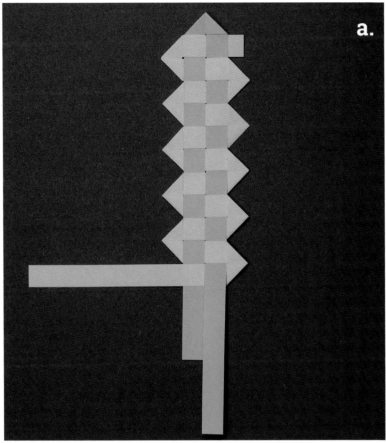

Braid trim made of an arrowhead and a continuous weft element

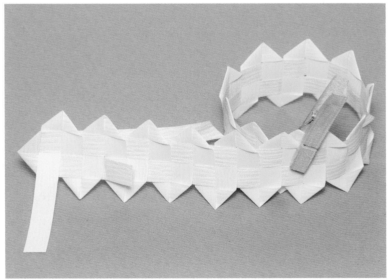

Braid trim made of gift-wrapping ribbons in two colors

Notes:

› In the example above, you are working along a horizontal working edge, and the finished weave is moving away from you—a comfortable way to work if you are working in small scale on a table.

› If you want to weave a very long mat or braid trim, it is more comfortable if the finished weave grows toward you; then it falls into your lap. Or you can sit on the growing weave as you work.

› You can also weave this type of braid trim using just one arrowhead as the starting line. [a]

› The weft element can also be wider or narrower than the strips used to make the arrowheads; the points formed along the selvage will then be larger or smaller than the arrowheads.

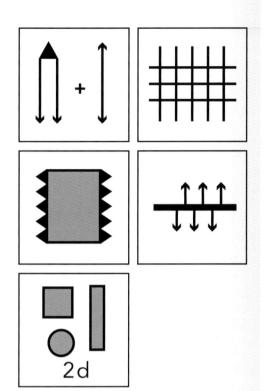

Materials

Single-ply paper strips, paper strips folded lengthways fourfold, gift-wrapping ribbons, natural material, etc.

Construction of a braid trim or mat of arrowheads with the finishing weft elements overlapping along a horizontal working edge, 1/1 orthogonally woven

This method works well for making mats or braid trim of all sizes. The number of arrowheads you use when starting the piece defines the width of the finished work; it can be as long as you wish.

The following steps describe how to make a braid trim when you start with three arrowheads:

› Place three arrowheads with pockets on the work surface so that the arrowheads point toward you. [1]
› Open the shed. [2]
› Place a new strip across the opened shed. [3]
› Fold the shed closed. [4]
› Open the new shed; the inserted horizontal strip will be held in place. [5]
› Fold over the end of the left cross-strip. [6]
› Fold it back over again right away; the end of the strip is now lying crosswise in the open shed. [7]
› Fold over the end of the right cross-strip over forward. [8] Fold it over forward again right away; the end of the strip is now lying crosswise in the open shed on the other strip end. The two strip ends should overlap by a few centimeters. [9]
› Close the shed [10] and open a new shed. [11]
› Insert a new cross-strip and continue to work. This creates serrated selvages on the braid trim.

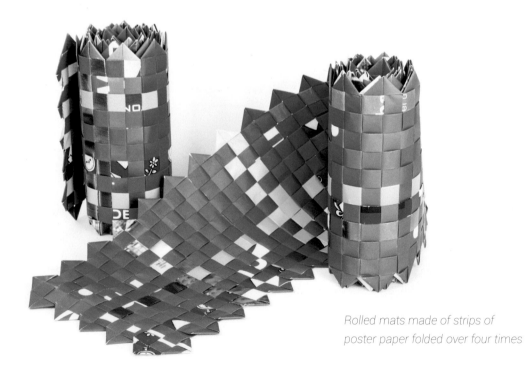

Rolled mats made of strips of poster paper folded over four times

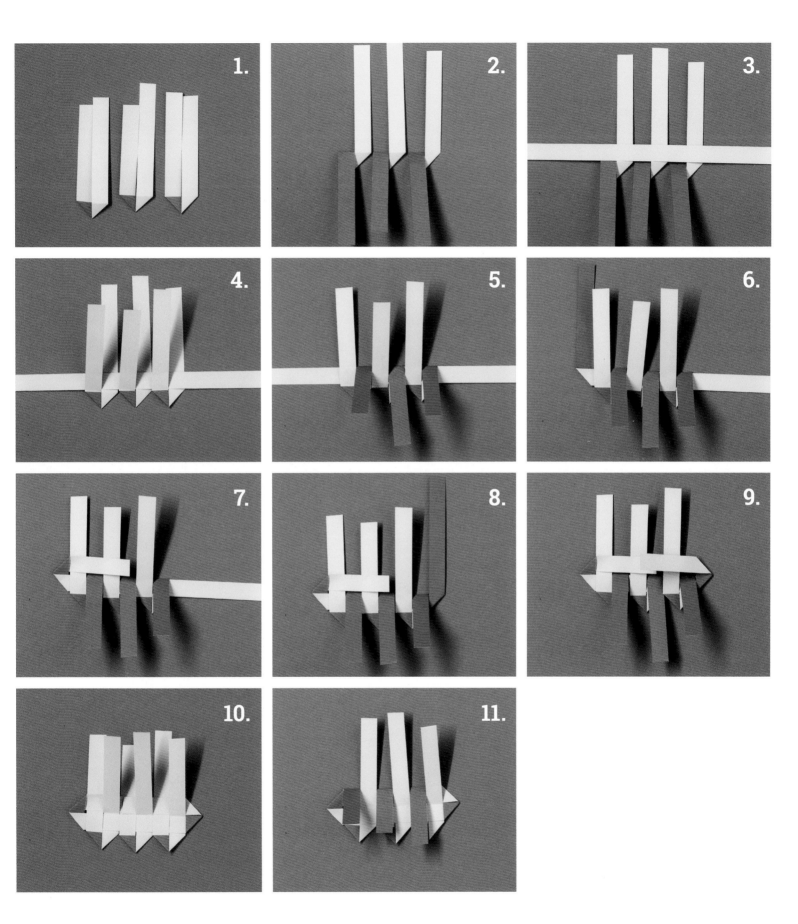

Notes:

› The inserted elements can be wider or narrower than the starting arrowheads.

› Since the weft elements are enclosed within the structure, there are no loose weaving ends at all along the starting edge and along the selvages.

› Again, the finished weave could grow in the other direction than that shown in the sample; to do this, start by laying out the arrowheads the other way around.

› A typical feature of this type of weaving is that it is always necessary to fold the elements over twice on one side edge and to fold them over backward on the other side edge, since there is always an even number of shedding elements.

› Folding over twice backward is usually considered more difficult and requires more precise work if you want to make exact points.

› It is necessary to keep lengthening weaving elements used to make the starting arrowhead by overlapping them. It's best to start off by folding the arrowheads so that the two ends are of unequal length.

Woven mats made of poster paper, exhibition in Lichtenfels, 2011

Woven mat of architect paper

Construction of braid trim from arrowheads without extra weft elements, 1/1 diagonally woven

To make this braid trim, start with two arrowheads. Because of the narrow width of the woven pieces, you can also work freehand, without using a work surface.

A characteristic feature of every diagonal weave is that you do not add any new material after you have set up the initial piece of work (apart from the fact that of course it is necessary to keep lengthening the individual weaving elements). Such diagonally braided trims are very elastic along the length and therefore work well if you sew them together to make surfaces and artifacts.

Below are three versions of diagonally braided trim:
1. **Flat braid trim:** This version can be found all over the world. Such braid trim is sewn together, for example, to make hats or bags. This braid trim is one of the few exceptions that can also be machine-woven.
2. **Twisting braid trim:** The second version is more of a plaything with intriguing features and effects.
3. **Braid trim with a ruffled edge:** The third version is mainly decorative and also known as a straw plait.

Braid trim made from two arrowheads, 1/1 diagonally woven along an A-shaped working edge, grass from the roadside

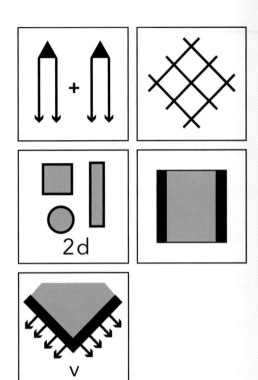

Materials

Paper strips, gift-wrapping ribbons, plant material, etc.

Variations:

› If you turn the side edges in a different way from that stated above, this will create a different weaving step. This will then look like a mistake and will not exactly match the required 1/1 weave. However, having such long weaving steps along the sides of a surface can be useful if later on you want to insert a rod, for example.

FLAT BRAID TRIM, WOVEN 1/1 DIAGONALLY ALONG A V-SHAPED WORKING EDGE

In the photos for the following weaving instructions, the loose weaving elements lie so that they point toward you. But you can easily work the other way around, along an A-shaped working edge. Once you have started, you can take the piece off the work surface and hold it in your hands to continue weaving. This is especially recommended for making very long braid trims, since you can then let the finished weave fall in your lap. This is the way that people have always done straw plaiting, for example.

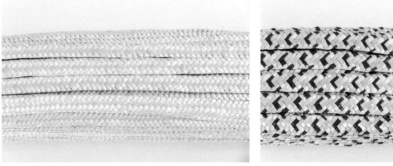

Bundles of plaited straw

› Start with two arrowheads. **[1]**
› Weave these two arrowheads together so that the pairs of weaving elements are interwoven diagonally. The interwoven arrowheads together form the horizontal starting line for the weave. The working edge is V-shaped. Make sure that you are really creating a 1/1 woven surface; that is, one strip always runs alternately over and under another one. The 1/1 weaving rhythm must also be maintained in the triangular areas. **[2]**
› Fold the outer yellow weaving element over forward **[3]** and then place it under the other yellow weaving element. **[4]** Now three weaving elements are pointing to the right.
› Fold over the yellow element of the group of three and form a shed. **[5]**
› Fold over the blue outer right weaving element backward and insert it in the open shed. **[6]**
› Close the shed. You are now back at the starting situation again, with a V-shaped working edge. **[7]**
› Repeat these working steps and make the weaving elements longer as required.

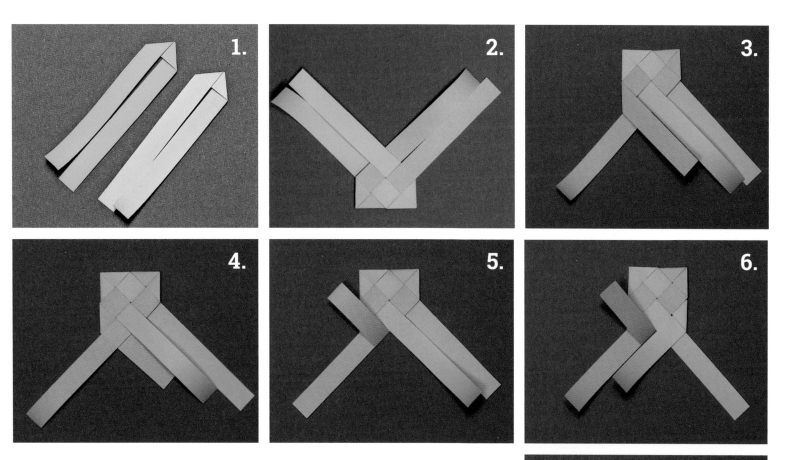

Notes:

› The working process will be familiar to you from hair braiding: once from the left, once from the right, and so on. However, braiding hair usually involves three strands; that is, an odd number of weaving elements.

› To work with an odd number of weaving elements (for example, for patterns with symmetries), you can use a "trick" when starting work with arrowheads: as you can see in the photo, you can work with a single strip instead of an arrowhead as the left corner of the finished weave (later you will work the ends back into the finished weave). [8]

› Working with an odd number of weaving elements allows you to always fold both strips the same way at the side edges.

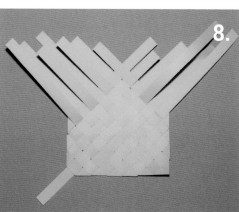

Growing braid trim made of two arrowheads, woven diagonally using gift-wrapping ribbon

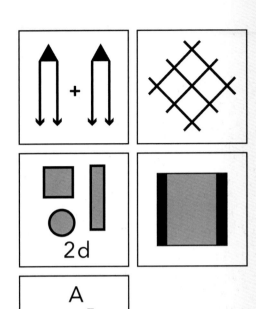

Materials
Paper strips, gift-wrapping ribbon, plant materials, plastic strips, etc.

TWISTING BRAID TRIM, WOVEN 1/1 DIAGONALLY ALONG AN A-SHAPED WORKING EDGE

This is a fun variation of the flat braid trim, which shows how intriguingly different a result you can get simply by working in a slightly different way as you weave. When working with two-colored paper, the growing braid trim always has the same color on the top side.

› Start with two arrowheads, as when making the flat braid trim.
› Weave these two arrowheads together so that the pairs of weaving elements are interwoven diagonally. The following photos for the weaving instructions show the loose weaving elements pointing away from you.
› The interwoven arrowheads together form the horizontal starting line for the weave. The working edge is A-shaped.
› Take the weave you started on the table in both hands.
› Now pass the outermost strip on the right, without folding it, under the second strip on the right; you have three strips of the same color in your left hand, and you can see a clear curvature emerging on the right. **[1]**
› Pass the outermost left strip of the group of three, without folding it, over the middle one of the group of three and under the last one of the group of three. The curvature is even more marked and there are again two weaving elements lying on each side. **[2]**
› Now keep repeating these two working steps. **[3 and 4]**
› The result is a three-dimensional braid trim that twists completely by itself. **[5]** Leave room to the left for the growing braid trim so that it can twist its way out of your hand. (You might want to help it along a little at the beginning.)

Twisting braid trims, made of the widest range of materials

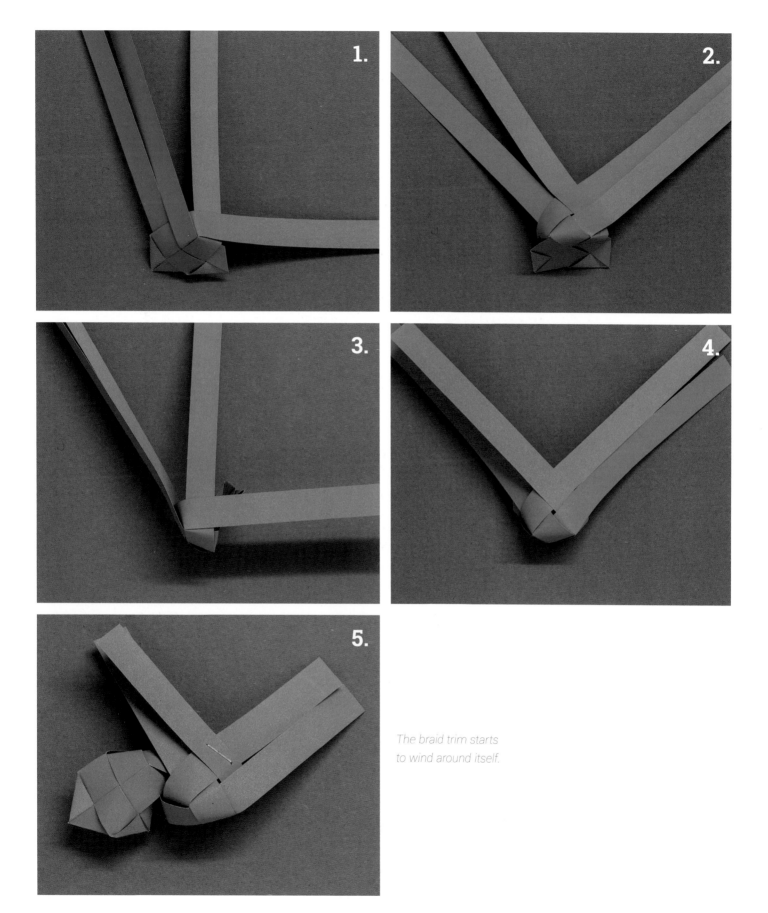

*The braid trim starts
to wind around itself.*

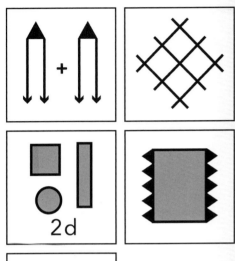

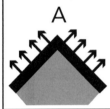

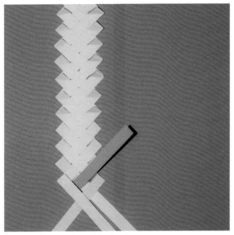

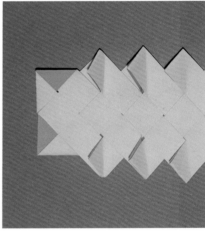

Materials
Paper strips, gift-wrapping ribbon, plant materials, plastic strips, etc.

BRAID TRIM WITH RUFFLED EDGE, WOVEN 1/1 DIAGONALLY ALONG AN A-SHAPED WORKING EDGE

In this version made of two-color strips, you likewise always have the same color on the top side of the braid trim. The selvages of the braid trim do not lie flat but, rather, stand up, which—depending on the material—can create either a stiffer or more pliable ruffled effect.

Braid trim with ruffled edge

Ruffle along one side edge

› Start with two arrowheads, as when making the flat braid trim. The working edge is A-shaped, the weaving elements facing away from you (two in the Z direction, two in the S direction).
› The two outermost strips on the left and right create the ruffled effect: to do this, first fold the outer S-direction strip over forward in the direction of the starting edge (as if you were taking one step backward). **[1]**
› Then fold the same strip over forward again, so that it now lies parallel to the two Z strips (Z groups of three); this forms a point facing upward along the side edge. **[2 and 3]** Now open a shed in the Z group of three to the right and, working with the outermost Z element on the right, take one step backward and then insert the strip in the open shed.
› Close the shed. Now you are back where you started, and the game starts again on the left side.

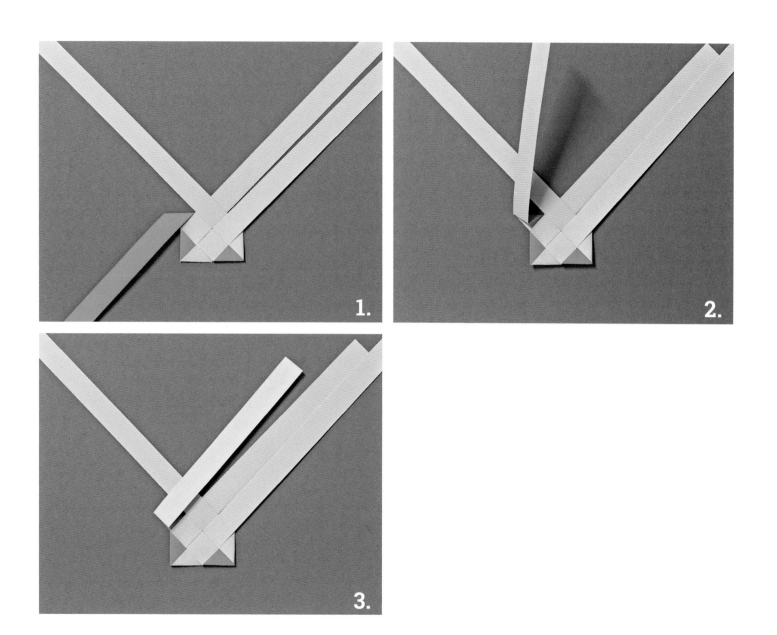

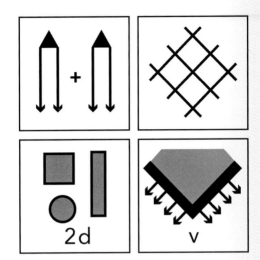

Variations:

> Select a different weaving stroke for the side edges (when turning, instead of folding over forward, fold over backward and vice versa) so that, for example, you can later insert a rod (see page 54).

> First stretch a basting thread on the work surface, then proceed as described above, but at the beginning work only with half arrowheads. Start on the side edges only when you have lined up all the half arrowheads on the basting thread.

> Change to a cross-grain working edge, so that, for example, you can create a twill pattern or a finished edge.

Start and construction of a larger surface using whole and half arrowheads, 1/1 diagonally woven

For the starting line you need one whole arrowhead and any number of half arrowheads. You can decide how wide the weave should become during the starting phase. In the photos, the structure is built up from right to left, but it can also be constructed the other way around.

> Start the right hand with an arrowhead; the pocket is on the right. Open the shed. [1]
> Take the first half arrowhead and place it to the left at the point of the starting arrowhead. [2]
> Close the shed. [3]
> Open the new shed. [4]
> Insert a new half arrowhead into the open shed. [5]
> Close the shed. [6]
> Open the new shed. [7]
> Insert a new half arrowhead into the open shed [8] and close the shed.
> Now you have reached the desired width.
> Open the new shed. [9]
> Form the upper left corner by folding over the leftmost weaving element (orange) forward and inserting it in the open shed. [10]
> Close the shed. [11] You have created a V-shaped working edge.
> Continue to weave in this way, once diagonally from the left, once diagonally from the right. As you do so, always fold over the outermost element on the side edge forward or backward and insert it in the open shed. The selvages form by themselves.

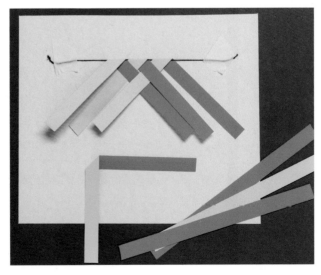

Starting situation with half arrowheads on the basting thread

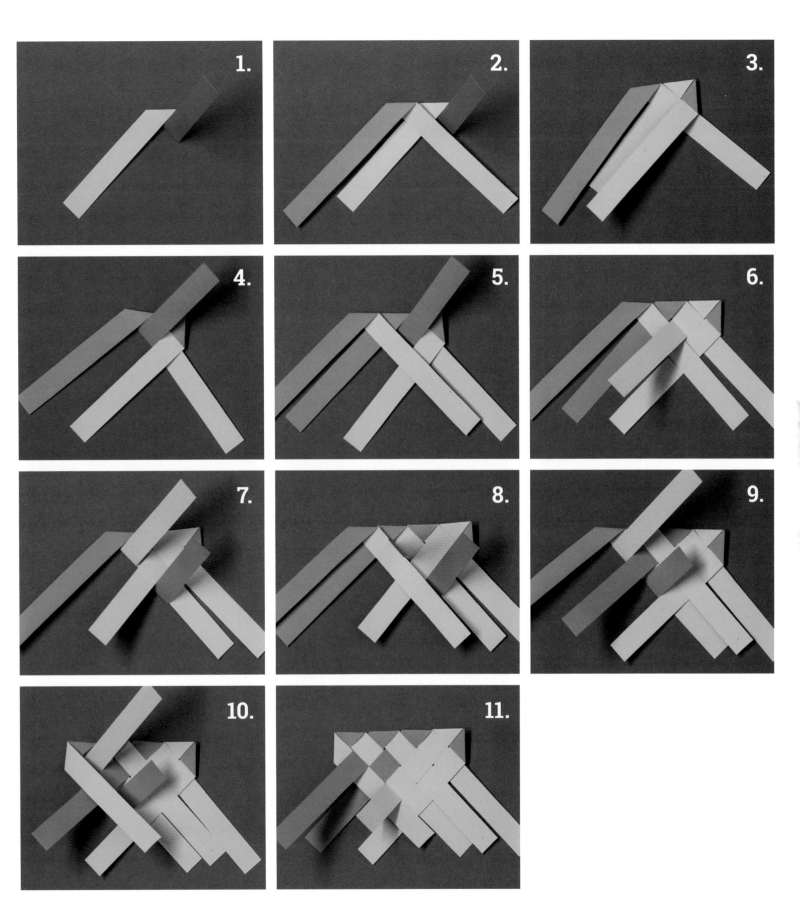

101

Construction of a braid trim, woven 1/1 in three directions

Not only is this design is elegant (hexagonal) and interesting because of the three directions the weaving elements go, but it also can be made very quickly and can be used versatile for use as a starting point: for braid trim, surfaces, and tubular or cylindrical objects.

This method works well for making braid trim of any length. It was also used in European regions in the past for plaiting straw. Similar braid trims are also found in Southeast Asia and Polynesia.

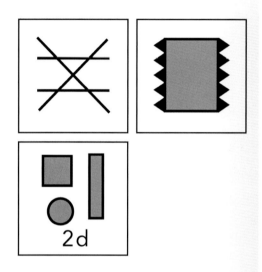

Materials

Strips of single-ply paper, gift-wrapping ribbon, natural materials, etc.

To start the braid trim, you need two weaving strips (in the sample presented here, in yellow and blue). Work as follows:

› Take the blue strip horizontally in your (left) hand and place the yellow strip underneath it at approximately a 60-degree angle. Fold the yellow strip around the blue strip so that the two yellow strip sections form a V shape at exactly a 60-degree angle. **[1]**

› Fold the right blue strip upward over the yellow to the left and place it parallel to the left, S-directed yellow strip. **[2]**

› Fold the horizontal left blue strip over backward and place it under the yellow S-shaped strips. Then pass this strip over the blue S-directed strip and place it parallel to the Z-directed yellow strip.

› At the beginning you had two strips. Now, out of these, you have created a clean hexagonal basic form with four weaving elements. **[3**]

Now the start is completed, and you begin constructing the braid trim:

› On the right side of the braid trim, you will see a small blue diamond shape. At this point, fold the right yellow strip over forward and insert it through under the left yellow strip to the left. **[4]**

› Move the yellow strip, now pointing to the left, in the same way once again. Fold it over forward to the top right **[5]**, and as you do so, insert it under the left blue strip, parallel to the right blue strip. **[6]**

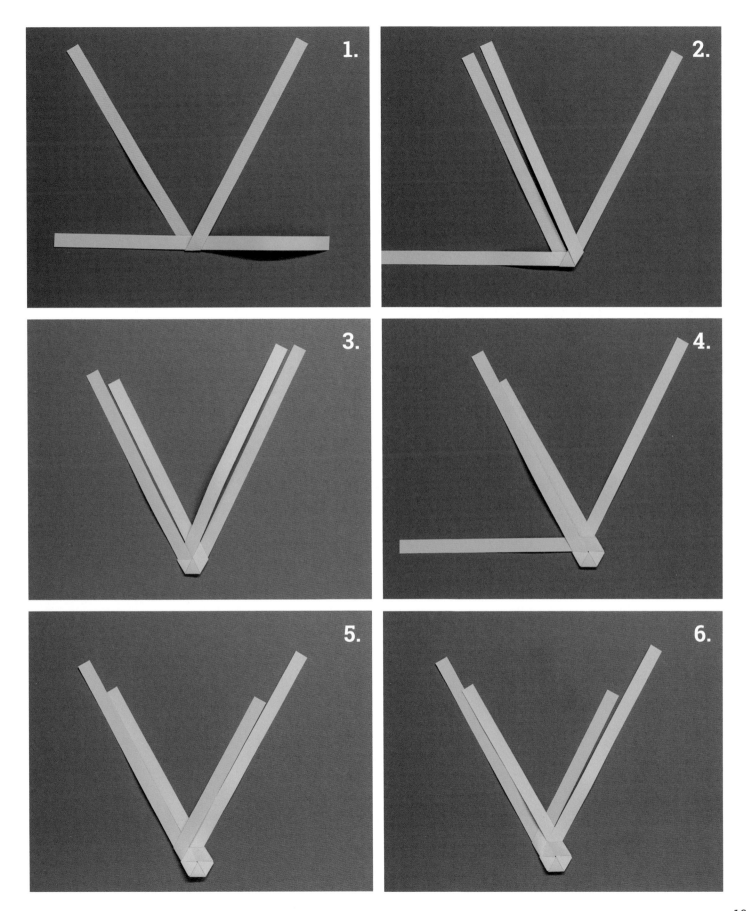

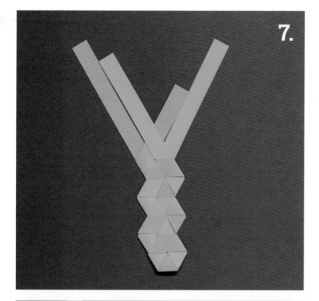

7.

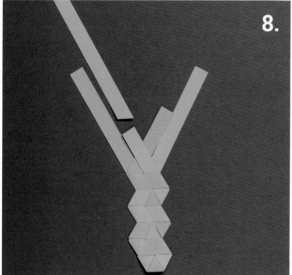

8.

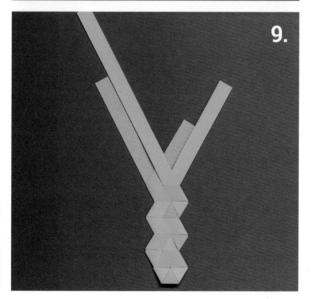

9.

› Now you can see a small yellow diamond shape on the left side of the braid trim. Proceed just as you did with the left yellow strip. First, fold it over forward horizontally and insert it either over or under the blue V-shaped strips to the right, then fold it over forward and insert it either over or under the parallel Z elements to the upper left, parallel to the blue S-directed element. Continue to work in this way.

› Make sure to maintain the over 1/under 1 weaving rhythm throughout; the lower middle of the V-shaped working edge is a key point for doing this. Keep in mind that with the respective weaving element you are working on, you should always work two steps in a row (one step horizontally and one step diagonally) before you leave it alone. The selvages become zigzagged.

› Figure 7 shows the growing braid trim. **[7]**

› Figures 8 and 9 show how the elements can be lengthened. **[8 and 9]**

Note: On page 122 you will find a way to finish this braid trim.

Braid trims made of natural materials. After weaving, they shrank up as they dried.

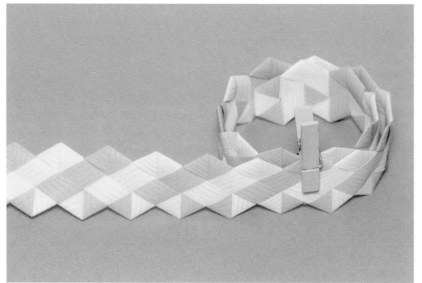

Growing braid trim made of gift-wrapping ribbon

Detail of a braid trim made of streamers

A braid trim made of saleen wicker to close a ring

Braid trim made of New Zealand flax (Phormium tenax)

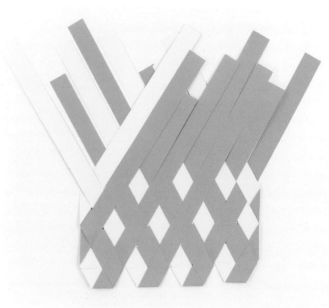

Constructing a surface with hexagonal starting elements

Variations

› You can mount the starting elements side by side, as shown in figure 3, thus creating a wider braid trim or surface. The variations of the working edges, selvages, and finished edges are the same as those for the diagonally woven braid trims shown at top above. You only have to get used to using more acute angles to weave the elements.

› You will get a braid trim with **straight** selvages if you turn the piece after each round instead of starting with once from the left and once from the right. Again, start with the round instead of at the small diamond.

› You can also have a lot of fun playing with the two versions of these braid trims by weaving alternately, using one or the other method within the same structure (zigzag selvage alternating with straight selvage).

› You can also simply stitch the braid trim woven in three directions together to form a large surface.

Sewing the three-directional braid trims together

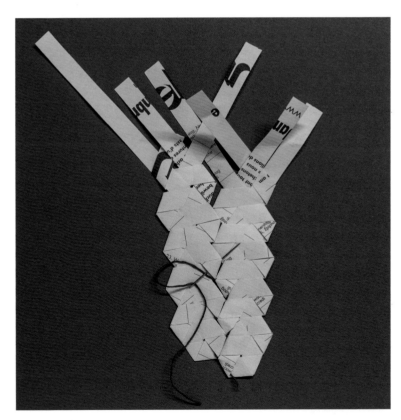

Start and construction of a diamond-shaped surface, orthogonally woven 1/1

You are working with one arrowhead and any number of other loose elements.

› Place the arrowhead on the table in front of you, with the point facing away from you.
› Open the first shed.
› Insert a strip horizontally in the shed. **[1]**
› Close this shed and open a new one.
› With the inserted horizontal strip, make a half arrowhead, one on the left and one on the right (folded over forward on one side, folded over backward on the other side).
› Open the shed where the new strip is placed. **[2]** Insert a new strip horizontally in the open shed.
› Close the shed and open a new one.
› Again, make two half arrowheads on the left and right sides, using the horizontal strips.
› Continue working this way until your surface is as wide as you want it.
› Make a full arrowhead on the left and right, using the strip you last inserted, and arrange it in such a way that the strip ends, now inserted horizontally in the open shed, come together and overlap inside the row—as when making the braid trim on page 91. **[3 and 4]** Continue to work this way until only the two lengthwise strips of the starting arrowhead remain. Use these to form a point, as described on page 125. **[5]**

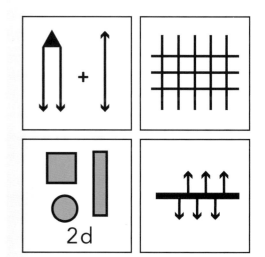

Materials
Single-ply paper strips, gift-wrapping ribbons, natural materials, etc.

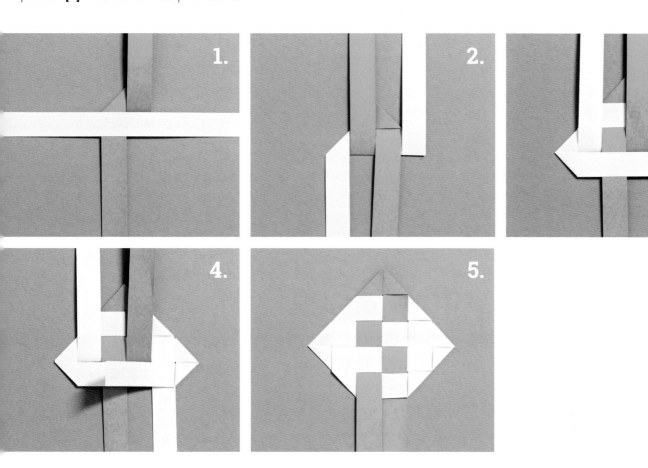

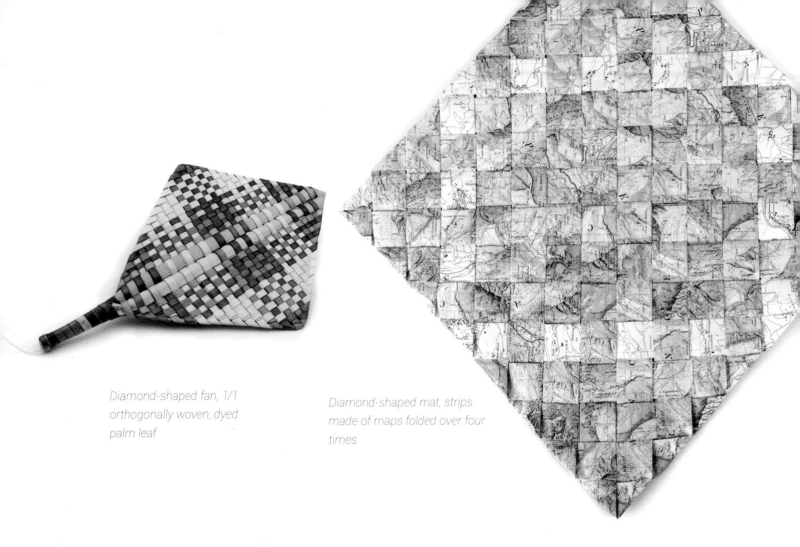

Diamond-shaped fan, 1/1 orthogonally woven, dyed palm leaf

Diamond-shaped mat, strips made of maps folded over four times

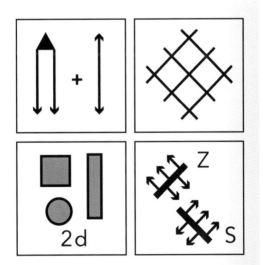

Variations

In my research, I have often discovered images and descriptions of mats that were started from one corner and then constructed diagonally. When you have reached the desired width for the mat, you then work on the second corner and continue to construct the surface without adding additional materials, as the diagonally woven surface described on page 101 is made. Due to the long passages on the S- or Z-directed working lines, this creates a strong cramming-spacing effect (see page 38), which gives rise to beautiful lines.

If you would like to try this process yourself, vary the work method described above so that the first arrowhead is at the bottom left and the elements lie on the diagonal; the mat grows toward you.

Combining starting situations—weaving a surface freestyle

You can combine and modify several of the starting positions presented above. You can insert additional weaving elements or reduce their number. You can insert slots, "bend" or turn the piece around as you like, make additional corners, combine ways to shape the edges—there are countless possibilities for weaving a surface freestyle!

FREESTYLE SURFACE

You can weave popular animal or other figures this way to make toys. Suitable materials for toys are single-ply paper strips, natural materials, and so forth.

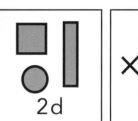
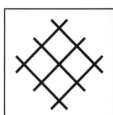

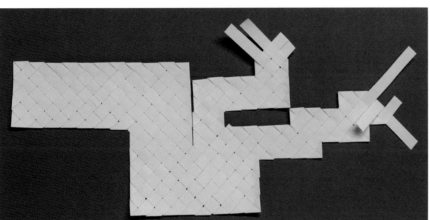

Freestyle surface, paper, 2d

Drawing an animal on checkered paper

Starting with Groups of Weaving Elements

There are three techniques for starting your weaving with groups:

1. Start with groups of pliable weaving elements with their ends tied together in a knot.
2. Start with groups of pliable weaving elements pulled in a bundle through holes in a prepared support.
3. Start with groups of very flat weaving elements that are "grown together" at one end (not yet cut through).

Bundled ends

For the first type, bundle together pliable strips, such as strips of fabric, bast, or paper tape tied or knotted together, and then weave them together under tension. Plaiting is the best-known example of this. Most of the braid trims presented above could also be woven from pliable strips with their ends bundled together. [1]

Bundles pulled through holes

I discovered an equally decorative and practical way to group a large number of pliable weaving elements into a starting position in a woven piece from the Cook Islands. Bundles of fine palm leaf weaving elements are pulled through holes in shell dishes and then arranged in pairs so that they can be woven diagonally. This creates extremely beautiful, precious base centers for making bags, containers, fans, and other things.

It is easy to test this work method by using a box.

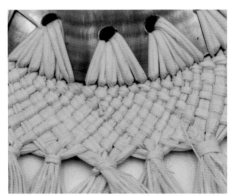

1/1 diagonally woven braid trim along V-shaped working edge made of bundles of paper tape

1.

Detail: Starting with bundles of palm leaf, using a shell as a "hole support," 1/1 diagonally woven, Cook Islands.

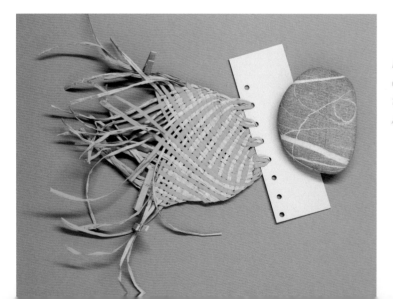

Experiment made of cardboard, strips of paper tape, 1/1 diagonally woven, A-shaped working edge

Groups of elements integrated at the base

I encountered this method in articles from the 1920s by Peter Buck / Te Rangi Hīroa. You work with groups of weaving elements that have "grown together" (integrated) at their base. I was immediately excited about this potential way to start a flat diagonal weave. In 1997, I visited the *Vanuatu* exhibition in Basel several times because the exhibit showcased this unusual way of working in detail along with many samples and photos. What I particularly liked was the fact that mats woven in this way are often made by groups of women who are sitting alongside the mat being woven at the same time. I found this social component attractive.

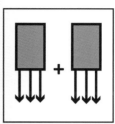

Pictogram: the elements are integrated at the base.

Characteristics:
› At the base, the individual weaving elements are joined together with several other elements as a flat surface.
› In this way, they form a group of adjacent, parallel weaving elements.
› The individual strips can be very narrow, which produces fine, pliant woven structures.
› Any parts of the starting edge that are still joined together when the piece is finished are either separated into individual elements and woven back into the finished weave or are left as a fringe.

It is interesting that the length of a finished mat is defined by the length of the starting side of the piece:
› After all elements have been assembled into the start position (*see below*), the resulting surface grows out of this to the subsequent width of the mat.
Instead of lengthening the weaving elements to make a mat of greater width, you can also set up a kind of second starting line on the resulting surface (see page 58).

Pandanus mat in progress, Wuro, West Ambrym, Vanuatu, © (F)Vb 32345: Museum der Kulturen Basel. Photo: Christian Kaufmann, 1983

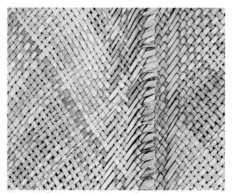

Detail of the original mat from Vanuatu

Two mats woven together, from Vanuatu

Sticky notes and paper strips

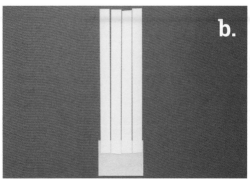
Four strips attached to the sticky area

Glue the adhesive strips over it. V + A 2d.

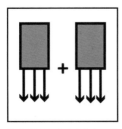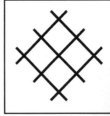

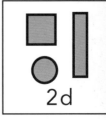

Materials

1 cm wide strips of DIN A4 paper with front and back of different colors

Preparing the materials

Instead of cutting wide strips into narrower ones, you can also work in the reverse way and paste narrow strips together into groups, such as by making several strips into a "sandwich" by using two sticky notes:

› Place a sticky note on the table with the sticky side on top. **[a]**
› Fasten the paper strips parallel to each other on the sticky strip. **[b]**
› Place a second sticky strip on top of the first one so that it covers the paper strips and the sticky part fastens the strips together again. **[c]**
› If you intend to work the ends of the weaving elements back into the finished weave later, you have to be careful to leave long ends when you paste the strips together this way.
› The number of strips per group can be even or odd.

STARTING AND CONSTRUCTION OF A SURFACE, 1/1 DIAGONALLY WOVEN ALONG A ZIGZAG WORKING EDGE

› Prepare the groups of strips as described above. **[1]**
› Now work with the groups lying along the diagonal on the work surface. Open a shed in one group; the strips can be easily folded back on the sticky note. **[2]**
› With a second group, fold back all but one of the weaving elements (on the sticky note at left). **[3]**
› Now weave the two groups together along the diagonal, as you already know how to do. In the sample shown, this creates small surfaces from 4 x 4 weaving elements. Here, I call these "packets." The weaving elements of the S-directed group are continuously connected to those of the Z-directed group. **[4–8]**
› Open another shed in one of the packets on the Z line and, using the method you already know, insert the first S element of a second packet into the open shed. The S element is tightly woven to the S elements of the first packet. **[9**]
› Close the shed, open a new shed, and continue to work until all the S elements of the second packet have been woven in. **[10–12]**

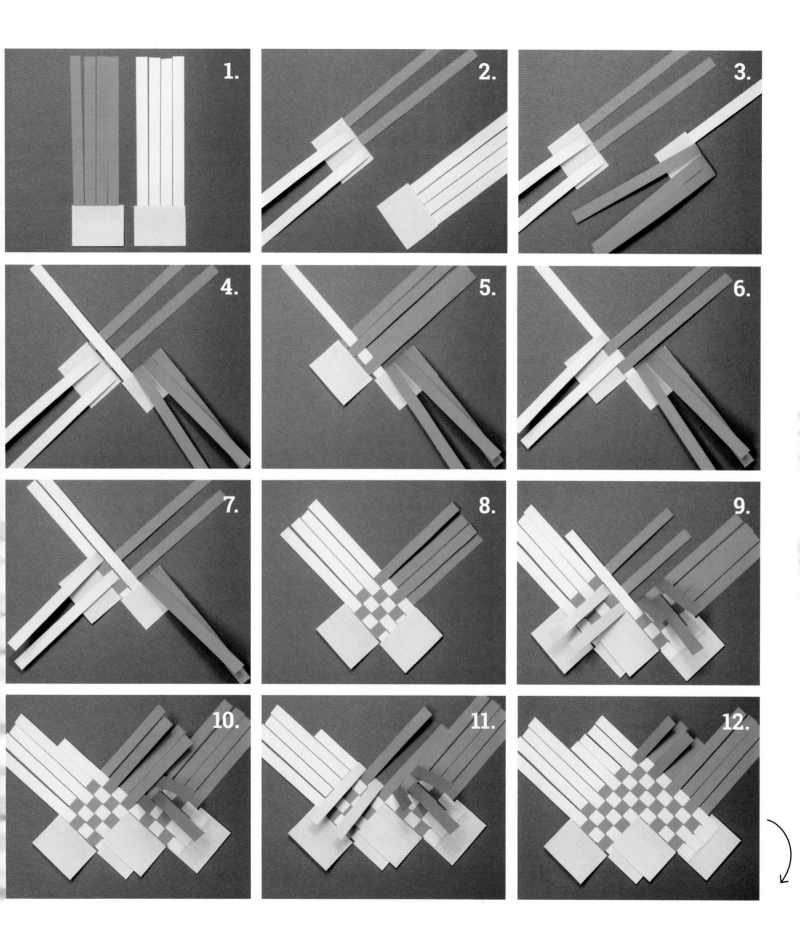

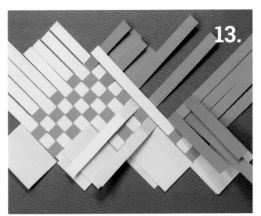

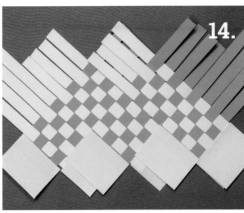

› Weave in a third packet: Open a shed made of four Z elements in the second packet and weave in the four S elements of the third packet. **[13 and 14]** Continue working in this way.

Notes:

› All packets have to be made in entirely the same way; that is, you must use an identical weaving rhythm. This can be clearly seen from the colors in the sample shown.
› Definitely always weave just 4 x 4 elements (or as many as your packets include each time). This is the only way to achieve a zigzag working edge.
› As soon as you have reached the desired width, start making the side edges. Definitely stay on the zigzag working edge, to avoid losing track.
› Make the weaving elements longer, either individually or as a whole group. **[15]**

Work in progress, mat made of calendar paper

Work in progress; two mats woven together, maps and magazine paper

Rolled, 1/1 diagonally woven mat of calendar paper, 40 x 600 cm

Starting Over a Solid Form

This way of starting work automatically creates three-dimensional artifacts. Working this way, you can make a tubular object by working over a cardboard tube, for example. The principle works for orthogonally or diagonally woven structures. The form is either used only temporarily as a support and is removed later, or it's kept in the finished piece.

Reproduction of a carrying ring, 1/1 orthogonally woven, saleen wicker, polystyrene ring

Tubing and basting thread to make a cylinder, 1/1 diagonally woven

Technique Group 2
Edges or Rims and Finished Edges

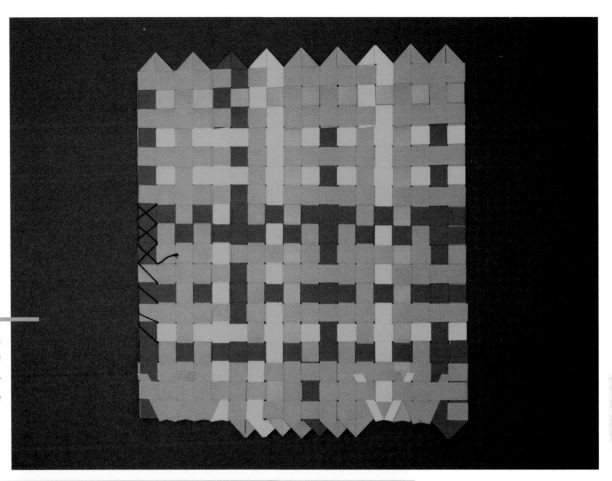

Work sample with edges fashioned along the diagonally woven surface

Work sample with edge fashioned along the diagonally woven surface

We can essentially distinguish two ways to create edges on woven pieces:

1. **Edges shaped while constructing the surface**
2. **Edges shaped after the surface is woven**

Here is an overview of the possibilities, shown as diagrams:

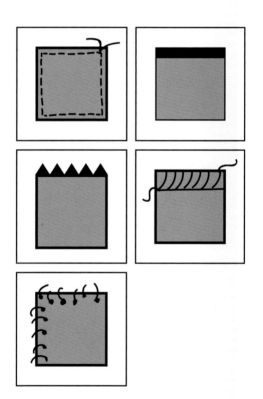

Edge shaped while constructing a surface

You have already learned about this category in "Technique Group 1." These include different starting edges as well as the integrated side edges (selvages) created as you construct diagonally or orthogonally woven structures (or both) using arrowheads; these may appear straight or zigzagged (see page 86).

Edge that is made after weaving the surface or artifact

It is necessary to shape an edge in places where there are element ends left over after you have woven your surface or artifact. These loose elements must be woven back into the finished weave and secured in this way.

This mostly involves finished edges, which are found at the top or bottom of surfaces or on top of three-dimensional artifacts. Less frequently, loose ends remain on all four sides of a surface. The diagrams show how the edge or rim is made on one side; as needed, just transfer to the other sides.

Note:

There are different techniques that will result in leftover loose elements along the working edge. Some are freely movable atop the finished weave; the others are held firm by the weave. In the following instructions, I'll call these either the "top-lying elements" or "underlying elements."

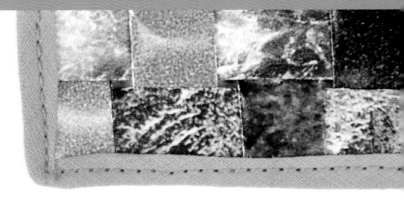

Details with machine-sewn seams

Linear **Finished Edges**

Orthogonally woven:

MAKING A STRAIGHT FINISHED EDGE WITH A SEWING MACHINE (OR WITH STAPLES)

This is an easy and quick way to secure the ends of loose weaving elements. The ends can be trimmed after they are sewn and left as is, or you can also cover them using bias binding, for example.

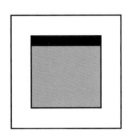

STRAIGHT FINISHED EDGE WITH LONG WEAVING STEP

In this finishing edge, the 1/1 woven pattern is slightly distorted. The paper in the sample shown uses two colors (front: yellow, back: green). This edge is made in two steps.

› In the first step, the underlying elements are worked back into the finished weave on the front side. When doing this, you have to do one weaving step over 2, so that the elements can even be woven into the finished weave. This looks like a mistake, but it's not possible to do it in any other way because of the orthogonal structure. **[1]** Turn the piece.

› In a second step, do the same with the remaining elements on the back side of the weave. **[2]** Trim the excess ends.

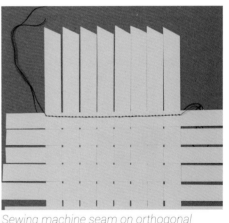

Sewing machine seam on orthogonal weave

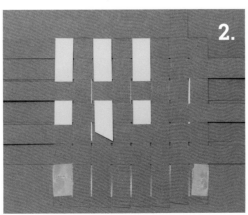

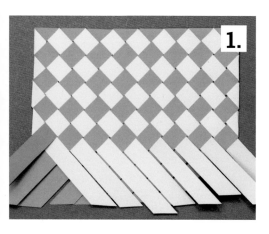

Diagonally woven:

To make any diagonally woven finished edge, first all the elements must be brought to form a cross-grain working edge; I call that "bringing the elements to the same level."

› The Z and S elements of each pair are at right angles to each other. Make sure that all pairs have the same element on top—either the Z or the S element.

› The paper in the sample shown uses two colors (front: yellow, back: orange). On the cross-grain working line, all the S elements are yellow and are "top-lying," while the orange Z elements are under the yellow elements. **[1]**

MAKING A STRAIGHT FINISHED EDGE WITH A SEWING MACHINE (OR WITH STAPLES)

Sew the seam before the ends are trimmed back. The trimmed ends can be left as they are, as shown here, or later covered over with bias binding, for example, or with extra elements. **[2]**

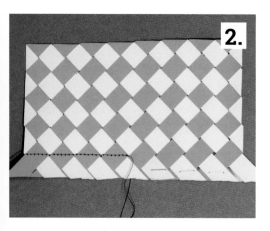

COMPACT STRAIGHT FINISHED EDGE

A stable finished edge that is woven in two work steps as follows:

› Starting point: cross-grain working line. To shape an edge, the piece is not turned around. Fold all the S elements over forward and work them back into the finished weave. **[3]**

› Fold the Z elements over forward and work them back into the finished weave. **[4]**

› Working the element ends back into the weave makes the surface thicker. Reinforcing it in this way can be very useful if you want to shape an edge.

› When working with two-color materials, this will not disrupt the color sequence.

› The farther the elements are woven back into the finished weave, all the more compact and thicker the edge becomes.

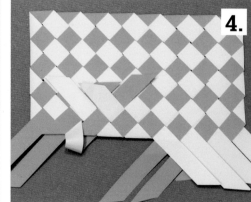

STRAIGHT FINISHED EDGE MADE OF SLANTED ARROWHEADS

Working with arrowheads slanted at an angle creates a decorative straight edge with a double row of slightly protruding squares.

› First, fold all the Z elements (shown here in orange) over backward twice and work the ends back into the finished weave; the color sequence does not change.

› Turn the piece. Because it was turned, the remaining elements show up again in orange and in the Z direction.

› In the second work step, fold each Z element over twice backward and work the ends back into the finished weave; the color sequence does not change. [5]

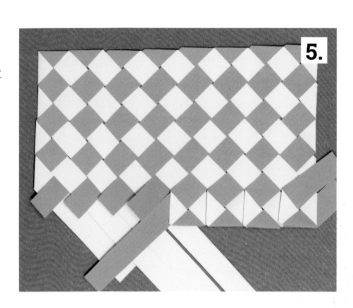

Finished edges on the outside of a basket

Variation

Instead of likewise folding a row of slanted arrowheads on the back side, you can also shape a normal straight edge there.

Finished edges woven in three or more directions:

If the weaving elements point in more than two directions, it becomes somewhat more difficult to find good solutions for making the rims. In open weaves, using extra elements works well (*see below*) or using combinations of straight rims and trimmed elements.

STRAIGHT FINISHED EDGE FOR A BRAID TRIM WOVEN IN THREE DIRECTIONS (PAGE 102)

It should be noted here that the woven elements were pointed in different directions when the weave was started—the elements were horizontal as well as in Z and S directions. I suggest working as follows:

> First position the weaving elements on the growing braid trim as shown in figure 3 on page 103 (outer S and Z diagonals are yellow).
> As usual, fold the yellow Z element over forward to the left, place it under the yellow S element, and leave it in the horizontal position.
> Fold the left yellow S element over backward and then place it horizontally to the right.
> Turn the piece and work all the weaving elements back into the finished weave on the back side of the braid trim as follows:
> Fold the yellow element over to the left, trim it, and tuck it into the blue pocket.
> Fold the yellow element over to the right, trim it short, and tuck it into the blue pocket.
> Fold the blue Z element over backward, trim it, and tuck it into the (first!) blue pocket.
> Fold the blue S element over forward, trim it, and tuck it into the yellow pocket.
> The sequence (above/below) should now be correct everywhere.

Straight rim on an open three-directional weave; the ends are worked back into the finished weave, combined with trimming them off.

Zigzag **Finished Edges**

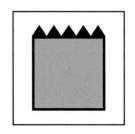

The material in the sample shown is yellow in the front and green in the back.

Orthogonally woven:

FINISHED EDGE OF WEAVING ELEMENTS WITH SPLIT ENDS

This process creates a decorative "**soft**" zigzag line. The edge is shaped in two work steps:

› In the first step, the underlying elements are worked back into the front side of the finished weave. Use a pair of scissors to split these elements up to the start of the finished weave. **[1]** Fold both parts forward and weave them, slanted to the left and the right, back into the finished weave. **[2 and 3]** Turn the piece.

› Do the same with the remaining elements on the back of the weave. **[4]** Trim the excess ends.

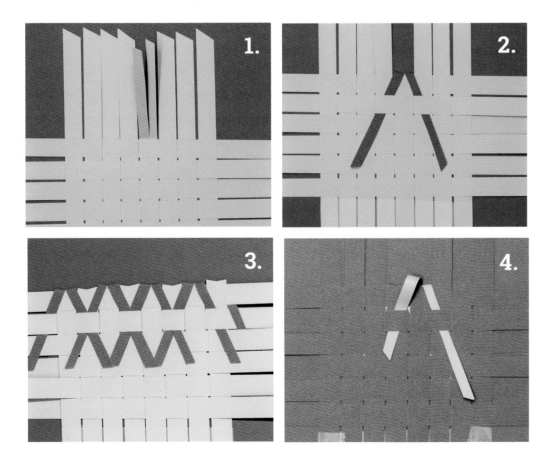

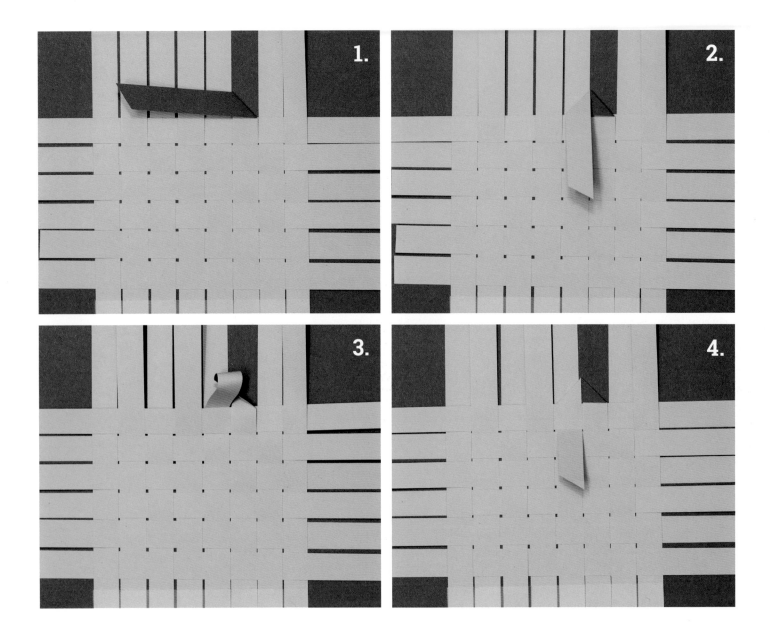

ZIGZAG EDGE MADE WITH ARROWHEADS

To make this edge, you work in two steps, using pairs of weaving elements:

› For the first step, you work with only the top-lying element of each pair. Pass a top-lying element in the direction of the "waiting partner" (to the left in the photo sample) by folding it over forward (half arrowhead). **[1]** Make sure that you are working along the line above the finished weave when making this fold.

› Fold the same element over forward once again in the direction of finished weave. **[2]**

› Then weave it back into the finished piece. You need to work a bit intuitively to do this. **[3 and 4]** Trim the excess ends. **[5]**

› Work the ends of all the pairs in a row back into the finished weave in such a way that the remaining "partner" elements are just left there for the time being.

› **Turn** the piece.

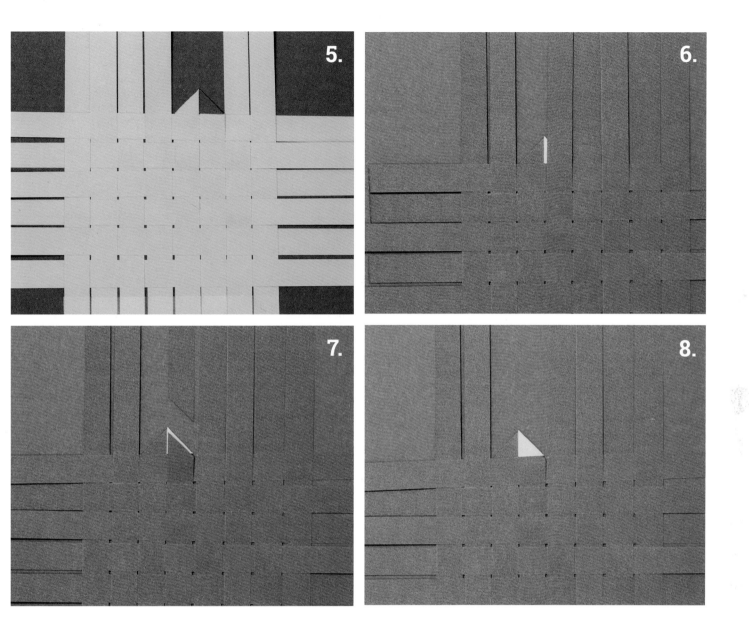

> Second, use scissors to trim the elements waiting on the back of the weave, and do this at the same angle as that on the points formed on the front side. **[6 and 7]**
> Insert the remaining short, triangular pieces into the pocket (yellow in the photo) on the point. **[8]**

Variations

Instead of cutting off the partner elements in the second step, you can use these to make the points in the same way as done on the front:

> If you work in the same way as done on the front side, the two points will lie exactly one atop the other.
> If you make the first fold to the right instead of to the left (as in figure 1), the new point will be offset from the one on the front.

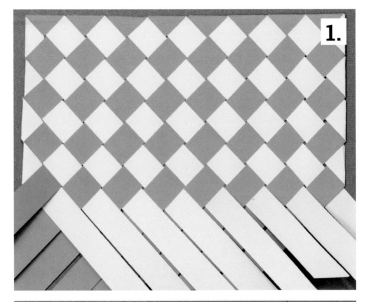

Diagonally woven:

You can also make serrated borders to finish a diagonally woven piece. The material used in the samples shown uses two colors: the front side in yellow and the back side in orange.

SIMPLE SERRATED BORDER

Each individual point incorporates pairs of weaving elements, consisting of one S element and one Z element lying diagonally one atop the other. This edge is shaped in two work steps:

› Place the work on the table with the back side facing upward (if there is a front and back); the working line runs across the grain. **[1]**

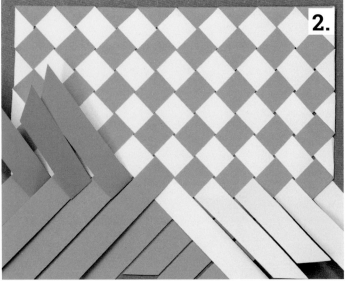

› First, fold the S elements forward over the Z elements **[2]** and work the ends back into the finished weave.
› Second, fold the Z elements over forward and work them back into the finished weave. **[3]**
› If using two-color materials, when you work the ends of the weaving elements back into the finished weave at least two weaving steps away, this creates a clear distortion of the color sequence created when working with two-color paper—this side should be the back of the piece. On the other side, however, the changing sequence of colors remains guaranteed.
› Instead of working in rows, you can also do the two steps, one right after the other, with each pair of S-Z elements lying one atop the other: First, work the S element ends back into the weave and then work the Z element ends into it.

Finished Edges with
Extra Elements

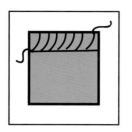

You can add extra elements to finished edges to cover any cutoff remnants; these also reinforce the work. The linear finished edges described above could also be used as a "veneer" to reinforce the edge.

Orthogonally woven:

This edge is made in three work steps.

› Work the underlying element ends back into the finished weave "over 2" on the front side of the weave. **[1]**
› Lay an extra strip over the top row in the weave. **[2]**
› Fold the "waiting elements" forward over this extra strip and work the ends back into the finished weave. [3]
› Trim the excess ends. You can also hem stitch the edge.

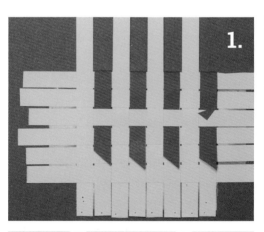
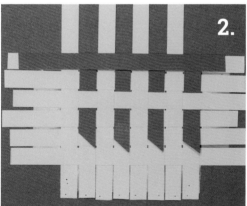

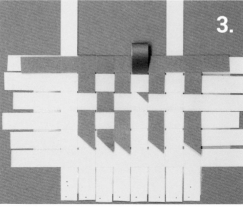

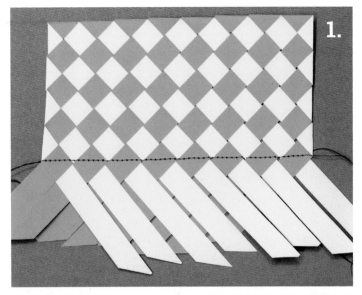

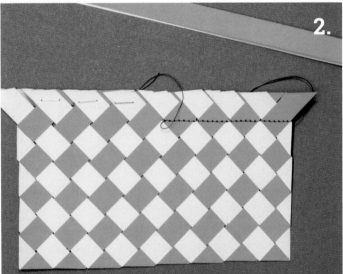

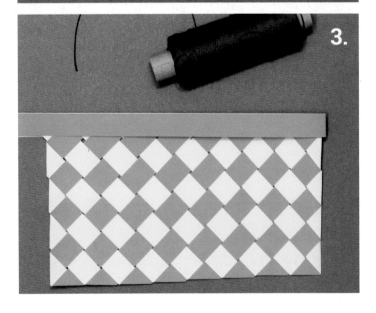

Diagonally woven:

This edge is made in four steps.

› First, secure the ends of the weaving elements by sewing them by machine, for example. **[1]**
› Trim the ends back.
› Place extra splints inside and outside along the trimmed ends **[2 and 3]** and secure them using clothespins or something similar.
› Last, fasten this arrangement using any good holding stitches— for example, you can use overcast stitches or cross stitches. You can use the holes in the finished weave to insert the needle.

Woven in three directions:

You have the same option of "veneering" an edge, using extra splints in pieces woven in three (or more) directions.

Whipstitched rim with various added splints in a diagonal weave

Freestyle **Edges**

Here are some suggestions for freestyle edging. You will certainly have some more ideas!

› Knot loose ends of weaving elements individually, in pairs, or in groups.
› If the material is very stiff, simply leave the loose weaving elements as is. You can also cut the ends off to irregular lengths, make them into a fringe, and so on.
› Finish the rim by using staples or glue.
› Turn the rim over or turn it upside down.

Small baskets with clamped and fringed rim, 1/1 diagonally woven, calendar paper

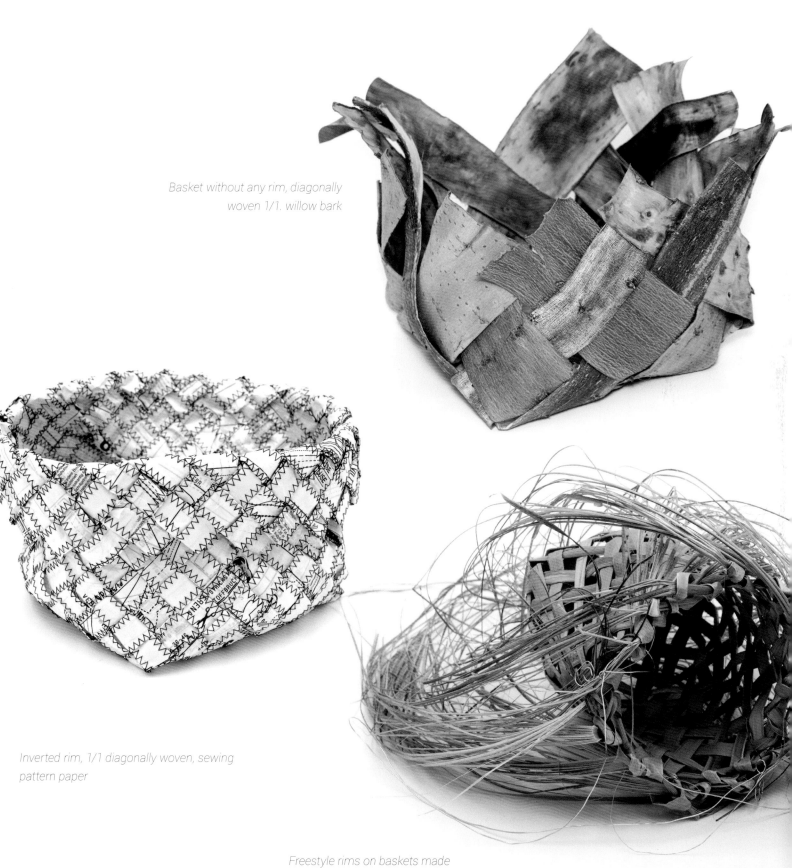

Basket without any rim, diagonally
woven 1/1. willow bark

Inverted rim, 1/1 diagonally woven, sewing
pattern paper

Freestyle rims on baskets made
of New Zealand flax

131

Technique Group 3
Three-Dimensional Objects

Using the basics from the first two technique groups, you can make wonderful three-dimensional objects—bags, baskets, cases, pipes, cylinders, or free-form objects. When making three-dimensional objects, you do not have to deal with the problems of constructing selvages, but then you're faced with a new challenge—giving the objects a specific spatial form.

1.

Basket and lid, 1/1 diagonally woven, twill pattern

Notes on the projects:

› The basket shapes presented in the following are so widespread that I will call them prototypes.
› For all the projects, there are alternatives to the indicated materials, strip widths, weaving rhythms, rims, colors, and decorative options.
› Baskets with lids are a combination of two baskets of different sizes, one fitting over the other. **[1 and 2]** These are similar to the bamboo case on page 19. There, the lid is a second, only slightly larger case.
› The following instructions are based on the explanations in the previous chapters. You can just page back if necessary.

CALCULATING THE LENGTH OF WEAVING ELEMENTS
› If you want to calculate the required length for the weaving elements for your own project, the best method is to get your bearings from the prototype and look to see the grain along which a single element is running (orthogonally or diagonally).
› Use a tape measure to measure some of the elements. In an artifact woven on the diagonal, the elements that form the corner are the longest.
› Convert these measurements to the desired size for your project and add 10–15 cm (4–6 inches) on both ends to make the rim and to have enough to work the element ends back into the finished weave.

Basket with attached lid, saleen band, 1/1 diagonally braided, straight end edges

2.

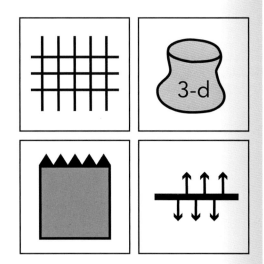

Materials

India-design wrapping paper from a museum shop, sheet size about 76 × 56 cm (30 × 22 inches), in two colors.

To make a basket with a 12 × 12 cm base (4.7 × 4.7 inches) and 16 cm (6.3 inches) high, you will need:
> 6 strips in one color, each 2 cm (0.8 inches) wide and 76 cm (30 inches) long
> 14 strips in a second color, each 2 cm (0.8 inches) wide and 76 cm (30 inches) long

If you follow these instructions, the weaving elements will be as long as you need right from the start, and it won't be necessary to lengthen them.

Orthogonally Woven Objects

Prototype A: Basket made of paper, orthogonally woven

The basket shown here can be a prototype for any type of orthogonally woven container. Despite its square base, the basket will automatically form a round rim at the top, unless you take strict care that all the weavers (weft elements) woven into the sides are always folded over at exactly the corner edges—which takes a lot of work.

BASE
› Weave a surface of 6 x 6 elements as shown in figure 1. I recommend starting from the center (see page 70), using shedding and clothespins at all four corners. **[1]**
› Secure the surface with one round of twining (see page 67). **[2]**
› Align all loose weaving elements to the same length.

SIDE
› You will need additional strips to construct the sides. First, "upset" (turn upward) all loose weavers (weft elements) once, along the basting thread.
› Prebend the weavers and corners, along the sides of the base. **[3]**
› Weave in the first weaver in 1/1, using the same pattern as for the base. Check that you are using the right weaving rhythm at the transition from the base to the side. The strip ends will overlap for a length of about 5–6 cm. The ends either point inward or are under an upright strip. Secure the round with clothespins. **[4]**
› Weave in the other weavers in the same way, arranging the overlapping areas in turn on all four sides in the process. **[5]**

RIM
To make the basket shown, work with the loose weaving element ends remaining outside to make a slightly serrated rim with split ends, as described on page 123. Inside the basket, work the ends back into the finished weave.

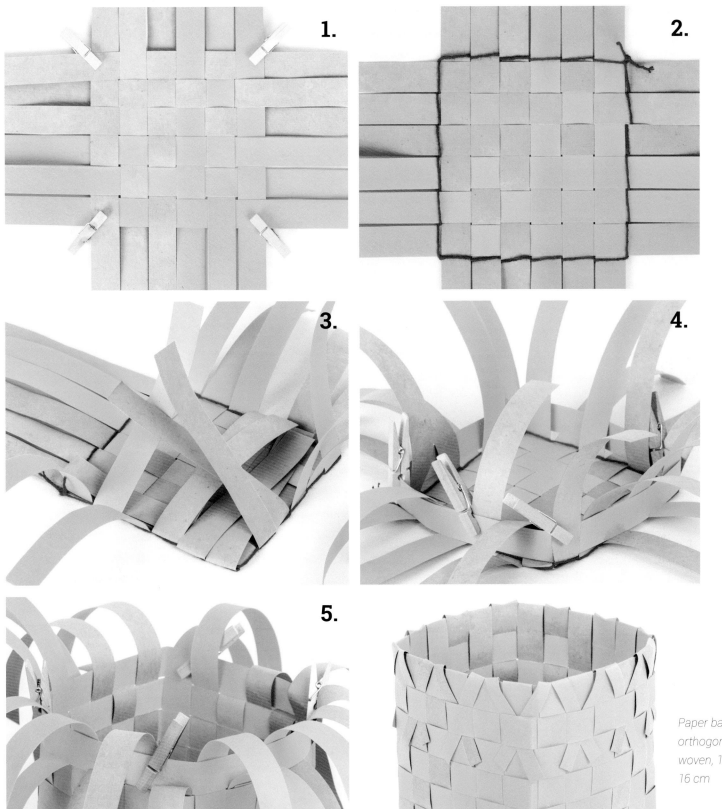

1.

2.

3.

4.

5.

Paper basket, orthogonally woven, 12 x 12 x 16 cm

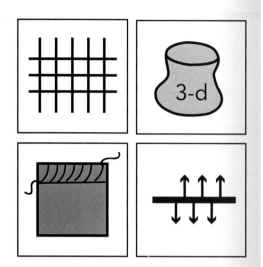

Materials

To make a basket with a 14 x 14 cm (5.5 x 5.5 inch) base and 13 cm (5 inches) high, you will need:

› 4 strips of drawing paper, each 2 cm (0.8 inches) wide and 42 cm (16.5 inches) long
› 3 strips of poster paper, each 2 cm (0.8 inches) wide and about 60 cm (23.5 inches) long
› 1 strip of poster paper, 4.5 cm (1.8 inches) wide and about 60 cm (23.5 inches) long
› 2 strips of saleen wicker, each 2 cm (0.8 inches) wide and about 60 cm (23.4 inches) long
› 1 strip of saleen wicker, 2 cm (0.8 inches) wide and 54 cm (21 inches) long
› 1 strip of poster paper, cut with pinking shears, 1.5 cm (0.6 inches) wide and about 54 cm (21 inches) long
› 4 paperclips
› remnant of cotton thread to secure the base and finished edge
› double-sided tape

If you follow these instructions, the weaving elements will be as long as you need right from the start, and it won't be necessary to lengthen them.

Handle basket made of paper and saleen wicker

BASE

› Weave a square base, using the 14 strips of drawing paper. I recommend starting from the center, using shedding and clothespins on all four corners.
› Secure the base using basting thread; the thread will remain in the basket as a decoration.

SIDE

› Construct the sides as done for prototype A
› First weave in the three narrower strips, then the wide strip.

RIM

› First trim all ends to about 2 cm (0.8 inches) long.
› Use two strips of saleen wicker to veneer these ends, as described on page 127, and stitch over them with decorative stitches of cotton.

HANDLES

› Place the serrated strips of poster paper on the saleen wicker and fasten them at a few spots by using double-sided tape (normal adhesive does not stick to saleen).
› Decide where to position the handle on the basket.
› Weave the handle into the side.
› Fasten the handle to the basket on both sides with two paperclips eachAttach the handle to the basket on both sides with two paper clips.

Variant of the basket with handles made of plastic hose and poster paper, quadruple folded; finished strip width: 4 cm

Handle basket made of paper and saleen wicker, 14 x 14 x 13 cm (measured without handle)

Handle basket made of spruce woodchip

Variation

The handle basket base may, of course, be rectangular instead of square. Then the upper basket opening will be oval.

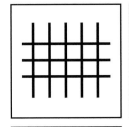
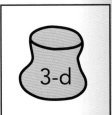
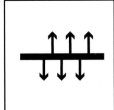

Materials

› Gift-wrapping paper in two colors
› 4 strips in both colors, each 2 cm (0.8 inches) wide and about 40 cm (15.7 inches) long
› Remnant of cotton yarn to secure the base

If you follow these instructions, the braiding elements will be as long as you need right from the start, and it won't be necessary to lengthen them.

Bag-like basket based on a Kapingamarangi design

This sophisticated woven structure can easily be folded out into a bag. I found the instructions for this in an ethnographic report about the Micronesian atoll Kapingamarangi. Fisherman's hats are woven in this way on the island.

BASE

› Make a surface of 4 x 4 weaving elements, as we did for prototype A on page 134. Arrange the strips so that about a quarter of the strip length is left on the left side, and about half the strip length is left on the right side as loose ends.
› Secure the surface with one round of twining (see page 67). [1]
› Note the position of the red dot in figure 1.

SIDE

› Here's trick that, in my opinion, makes the further weaving work easier. Turn the whole piece with the shorter ends of the loose weaving elements pointing to the left and upward, and the longer ones to the right and downward. (The red dot is now hidden on the strip that runs out of the finished weave on the lower right edge.)
› Bend all long elements—shown in sun yellow in the picture—over onto the finished woven surface. [2]
› Now weave the long blue elements, one after the other, into the bent-over yellow elements. Make sure that you are using the correct weaving steps and continuing the 1/1 pattern of the already woven surface (lift up your work slightly and check). This forms a case. [3 and 4]
› Secure the corner with a clothespin.
› Now you can reach into the case and carefully turn it out to make a bag.
› The new edges are now on the diagonal, and the loose ends of all weaving elements are lying one atop the other in the same direction (one color on the front, the other on the back). [5]
› Finish the work with any kind of rim you want, or continue to weave the structure in a cylindrical shape by adding extra elements. These should overlap in each round (as in prototype A on page 134). [6]

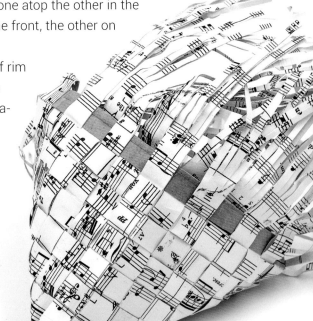

Single object from the wreath on page 57, music note paper, orthogonally woven.

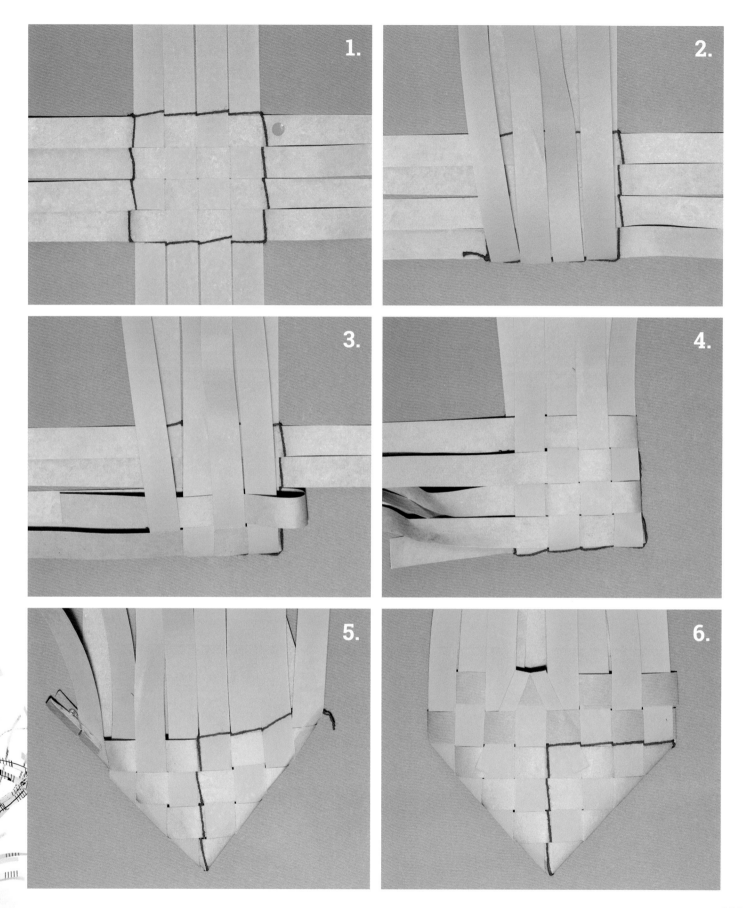

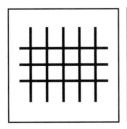
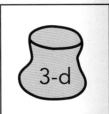
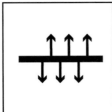

Materials

Many materials work well for making bracelets. Here I used ready-made paper tape that is woven over an insert made of saleen wicker.

› Saleen wicker, 22 mm (0.9 inches) wide and about 50 cm (20 inches) long (the length must match your wrist)
› Paper tape in one or several colors
› Adhesive tape
› Clothespins

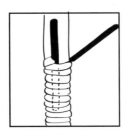

Making the wrapping fiber longer

Bracelets made of paper tape

On page 115, I mentioned the way to start work by using a solid form. This is the basis for making these bracelets; a ring of saleen wicker serves as the solid form. The bracelets shown have an inner diameter of 7 cm (2.75 inches).

PREPARING THE RING

› Make a ring of the saleen wicker (the ends should overlap slightly). To do this, adjust the diameter to your wrist.
› Secure the ring with a clothespin or some adhesive tape.
› First wrap the ring with paper tape to hide the saleen wicker and give the ring some extra volume.

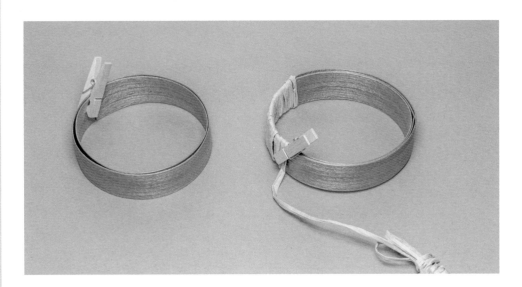

MAKING THE FIBERS LONGER

Note: In the drawing, the underside of the fiber is shown in dark color.

› Before you get to the end of the old fiber (about 15 cm—6 inches—before the end of the fiber), stick the new fiber—working on the underside of the ring—into the finished weave along the grain direction and parallel to the old one (underside up) and wrap them around together for about 5 cm (shown by dashes in the drawing).
› Then twist the old fiber together with the new fiber (its top side coming upward) and continue winding it over the ring along with the new fiber.
› In the process, wind the end of the old fiber (after twisting it together with the new fiber, underside upward) around along with it. The twisting leaves a small "bump" visible on the inside of the ring.
› Keep the winding fiber long enough so that you can use it as a weaving fiber when you have finished the winding process.

Bracelets made of paper tape, various patterns, orthogonally woven

WEAVING A BRACELET

› Cut five colored elements to size lengthwise. The length should correspond to the size of the bracelet plus about 1.5 cm (0.6 inches) extra.
› Insert the five lengthwise elements side by side under the winding fibers at any point on the bracelet and secure with a clothespin (do not glue them).
› Now use the winding fiber as a weaving fiber to make an orthogonal weave; do not weave the inside of the ring.
› Open a shed using the five lengthwise fibers, according to the desired pattern. This is the same technique you'd use when making an orthogonally woven braid trim, but you do not have to make any selvages.
› Insert the weaving fiber in the open shed and pass it around the ring once.
› Close the shed and open a new shed. Continue working in this way and, if necessary, lengthen the weaving fiber as described above. While wrapping and weaving, arrange the lengthwise elements in a nice pattern along the width of the carrier ring.
› Toward the end you have to keep a close eye on the remaining distance to the start of the piece so that the pattern fits perfectly.
› Use a blunt sewing needle to guide the ends of the lengthwise fibers a little way over the starting fibers, in the same pattern.
› Work the weaving fiber back into the finished weave on the underside of the ring, and secure with glue if needed.

Variations

› Instead of weaving the beginnings and ends of the lengthwise elements one atop the other, wind the remaining weaving fibers over the beginning and end sections without following a pattern.
› Search for patterns in books about handle baskets.
› If you make a bracelet with fresh or damp natural materials such as grasses, iris leaves, or flat rattan reed, you should allow it to dry on a glass or a bottle of the appropriate size after you have finished weaving. This gives the bracelet a nice shape.

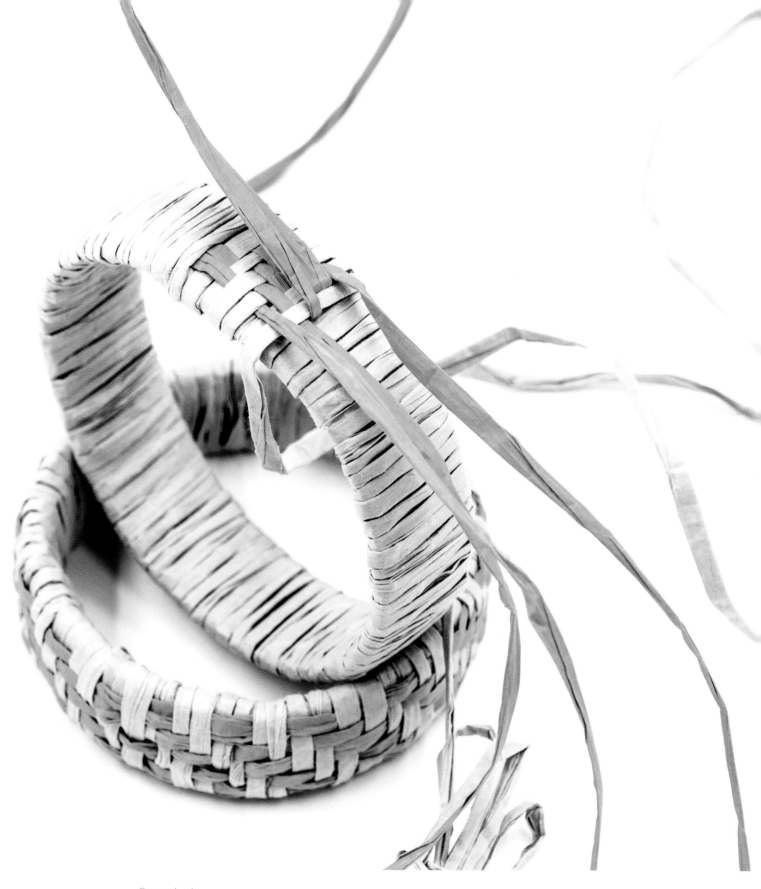

Open shed

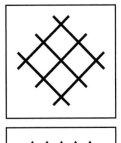
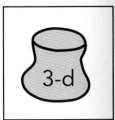

Materials

› Gift-wrapping paper, about 76 x 56 cm (30 x 22 inches), in two colors

To make a basket with a 12 x 12 cm (4.7 x 4.7 inch) base and 16 cm (6.3 inches) high, you will need:
› 8 strips in one color, each 2 cm (0.8 inches) wide and 76 cm (30 inches) long
› 8 strips in a second color, each 2 cm (0.8 inches) wide and 76 cm (30 inches) long
› cotton yarn scraps to secure the base
› clothespins

If you follow these instructions, the weaving elements will be as long as you need right from the start, and it won't be necessary to lengthen them.

Diagonally Woven Objects

Diagonally woven three-dimensional objects are really impressive, because once you start and have woven the first surface, you do not have to add any new materials at all. This is an efficient method for making baskets that is widely used all over the world.

Prototype B: Paper basket, diagonally woven

The basket shown here serves as a prototype for any kind of diagonally woven container.

Despite its square base, the basket will automatically turn out round at the top rim, unless you are working over a solid form.

Paper basket, diagonally woven, 12 x 12 x 16 cm

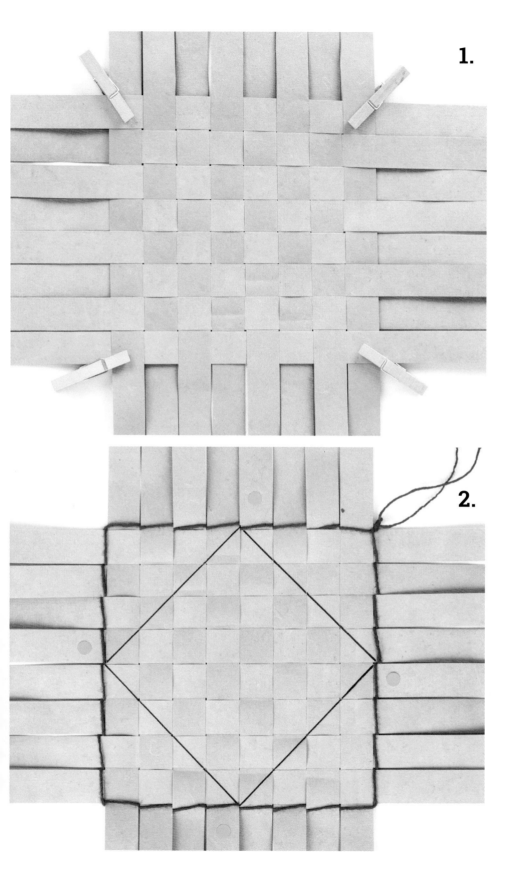

1.

2.

BOTTOM PIECE

› Weave a surface of 8 x 8 elements as shown in figure 1. I recommend starting from the center, using shedding and clothespins on all four corners. **[1]**
› Secure the surface with one round of twining (see page 67). **[2]**
› Align all weaving elements to the same length. The future base lies like a square on one tip within the just-woven bottom piece (you can mark it as in figure 2). Unlike the orthogonally woven basket, the corners of this diagonally woven basket will be formed each time in the center of each of the four bottom piece sides; thus, parts of the bottom piece automatically already become parts of the basket side.

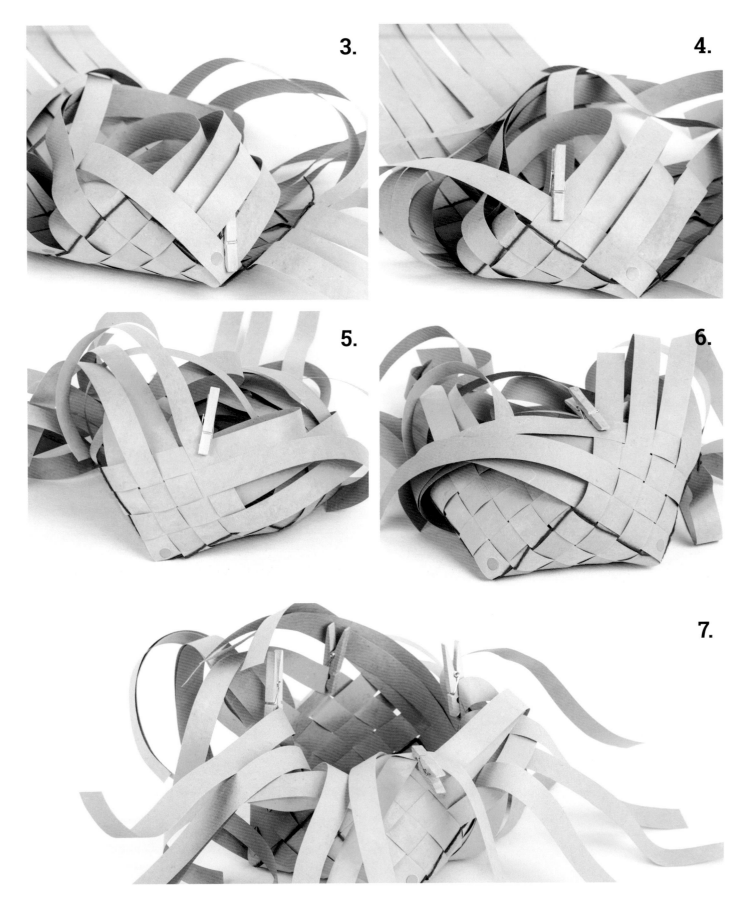

3.

4.

5.

6.

7.

CORNERS AND SIDES

In the process described below, the four corners and the beginning of the future basket side are woven in one work step.

› Place the piece either in your lap or in front of you on the table, in such a way that you are looking at what will become the outside of the basket. Have enough clothespins within reach.

› Start on any side of the bottom piece and make two groups of the still-unwoven strips. Hold four elements in your left hand and four in your right.

› Now interweave two groups with each other. If you wish, you can bend the two strips slightly over the basting thread, right at the future corner point. Fold the element in the right group that is farthest to the left (with the red dot) at a 90-degree angle over the element in the left group that is farthest to the right. Then secure with a clothespin. **[3]**

› Before weaving the strip all the way through the four elements of the left group, you should check whether the 1/1 sequence matches the bottom piece of the resulting basket. If this is the case, weave the strip all the way through and make sure that the strips at the just-formed corner are at right angles to each other. Secure with a clothespin. **[4]**

› Weave the other three elements of the right group to the left in the same way. Now 4 x 4 elements are interwoven 1/1 and at right angles. **[5]**

› Turn the piece clockwise or counterclockwise and again interweave two groups of four elements. Now the basket already has two corners.

› Again, secure the corner with a clothespin. **[6]**

› Shape the remaining two corners of the basket in the same way. Now the whole thing is already clearly three-dimensional, and you have created four solid-colored surfaces. The working edge is a zigzag all around. **[7]**

› Now look for the areas where you can once again recognize two groups of not-yet-interwoven elements. Again, take four elements in the left hand and four in the right. Interweave them; the colors will get mixed together again. Be very careful that you are really only interweaving 4 x 4 elements each time. Keep working in this way along all the sides. There may be some cramming-spacing effect in the structure, as described on page 38, with looser and more tightly woven parts alternating.

RIM

The basket shown has a simple serrated rim, as described on page 126. To make this, first bring all weaving elements to one height (see page 120) and shape a finished point with each pair of diagonals.

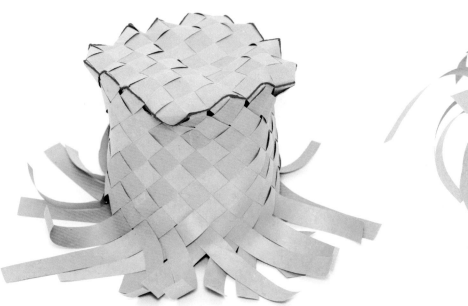

Basket with "zigzag-corner base," view of the base

Basket with "zigzag corner base"; the rim still has to be made

Variations

The container with a lid on page 19 inspired me to create an unusual version of the transition from the basket base to the side. Shape corners around the entire bottom piece, using two adjacent strips each time. To do this, you need to start out with a lot of clothespins! Then weave again in sections, using 4 x 4 elements, and end with a zigzag working edge as described above.

Detail of the transition from the base to the side on the container on page 19

Series of baskets, modifications of prototype B, paper, saleen, linden woodchip

148

Paper basket made of poster paper with fringe decoration

This is a wastepaper basket in the truest sense of the word! It is made in the exact same way as prototype B on page 144.

BOTTOM PIECE

› Weave a surface, using 10 x 10 elements. I recommend starting from the center, using shedding and clothespins in all four corners. This time, do not align the individual elements to the same length on purpose, so that when you lengthen them, not all the doubled sections will be at the same height in the woven piece.
› Secure the surface with a round in twining as described on page 67.

CORNERS AND SIDES

› Make the corners and sides as done for prototype B.
› Lengthen the elements where necessary, keeping the strips overlapping by about 8–10 cm (3.14–4 inches), and secure them with double-sided adhesive tape.

RIM

› Once you have reached the desired height (the shortest element specifies this), bring all elements to the same height (see page 120).
› Weave a finished edge, alternating between a serrated rim and a straight rim as described on pages 120 and 126.
› Use scissors to trim the weaving elements, which were worked back into the finished weave, into a fringe on the sides.

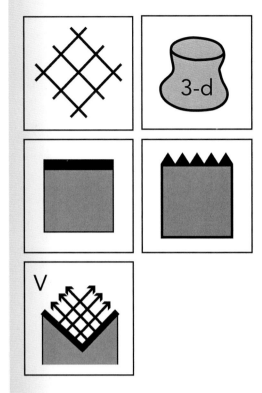

Materials

Poster paper, 4–5 sheets of about 90 × 128 cm (35 × 50 inches)—paste 2 sheets of each together with paste, printed side facing outward

To make a basket with a 24 × 23 cm (9.5 × 9 inch) base and 42 cm high (16.5 inches), you will need:
> 60 strips, each 3 cm (1.2 inches) wide and about 128 cm (50.4 inches) long
> double-sided adhesive tape

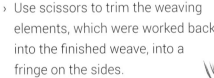

Paper basket of poster paper, diagonally woven, about 24 x 24 x 42 cm

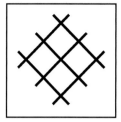
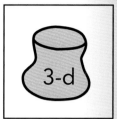
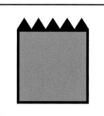

Materials

To make a basket-weave bag with
a base of about 20 × 36 cm (8 × 14
inches) and about 31 cm (12.2 inches)
high, you will need
› 34 saleen wicker strips, each
2 cm (0.8 inches) wide and 150 cm
(59 inches) long
› cotton yarn scraps to secure the
base

If you follow these instructions, the
weaving elements will be as long as
you need right from the start, and it
won't be necessary to lengthen them.

Basket-weave bag made of saleen wicker with bamboo handles

This is another version of prototype B on page 144; the bottom piece this time is a
rectangle instead of a square.

BOTTOM PIECE
› Weave a bottom, using 17 x 17 elements as described on page 70.
› Mark the rectangle for the future base.

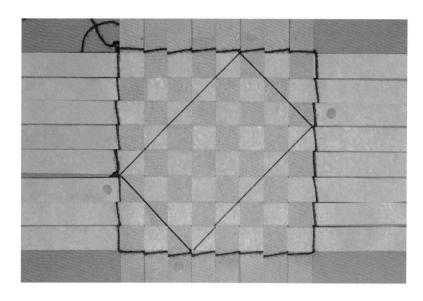

*Starting situation fc
the rectangular bas
for a diagonally
woven basket*

CORNERS AND SIDES
› In principle, you should proceed in a way very similar to the one used to make
prototype B, but you will not make the corners exactly in the center of each bottom piece side. On the two opposite sides, you have a group of ten elements on
the left and a group of seven elements on the right, and on the other two sides,
the left group consists of seven elements and the right group of ten.
› Weave the side until the shortest weaving element is still about 15 cm (6 inches) long.

RIM
› Bring all weaving elements to the same height (see page 120).
› Weave the serrated rim, while working the elements back as far as possible into
the woven side. Leave the ends about 3–5 cm (1.2–2 inches) long (they may be
irregular—that is, it isn't necessary that all end pieces are at the same height).
› Use scissors to trim all the end pieces into a fringe.

Basket-weave bag made of saleen wicker with bamboo handles, 1/1 diagonally woven, about 20 x 36 x 31 cm

HANDLES

To make this bag, bamboo handles were fastened into the finished weave. These handles have a crosswise metal bar, which you can unscrew to insert it into the weave.

Metal bar, inserted crosswise in the weave

Screws on the handle

Materials

Saleen wicker, 20–22 mm wide, in five colors

To make a basket with a 15 cm (6 inch) base diameter and 30 cm (11.8 inches) high, you will need:
› 2 strips in each of four colors, each 125 cm (49 inches) long
› 8 strips in a fifth color, each 125 cm (49 inches) long
› a piece of string for basting thread
› pins and a pad (cardboard, ironing board, or something similar)
› clothespins

If you follow these instructions, the weaving elements will be as long as you need right from the start, and it won't be necessary to lengthen them.

Round basket on a star-shaped base, diagonally woven

This version for a basket requires making the star-shaped base on page 83.

Basket made of saleen wicker with star-shaped base, diagonally woven

BASE

Weave a base according to the instructions on page 82.

SIDE

› This is where the eight strips of the fifth color (gray here) come into play. They form both the last part of the base weave and the eight corners of this basket at the same time, then they are turned into a part of the side weave.
› To shape the corners, cross two parallel-lying elements of the base star over each other and weave in a gray element in the process each time. Make sure that, when crossing the elements, you continue the over 1/under 1 weaving rhythm to match the base elements. Work in this way to make a total of eight corners. As you do this, the woven-in elements will now be at right angles to each other. Secure the connection each time with a clothespin.

› Bring the gray woven-in elements to an even length. Now you have worked all the elements you need to make a diagonally woven side into the base and have not added in any extra materials.

› The long strips make it more difficult to keep an overview. I therefore recommend that you first weave in two gray elements for one round and secure them using one clothespin each. This makes it easier for you to recognize which groups of weaving elements should respectively be interwoven together.

› You can weave the side by using an over 1/under 1 weaving rhythm throughout, or, as in my example, at a certain height you can switch to horizontal twill (see page 180). Bring all weaving elements to the same height, as described on page 120. Then continue weaving in the over 2/under 2 pattern in rounds.

RIM

The basket shown has a zigzag rim as described on page 126.

Variation

Here is another intriguing and playful version:

› Starting position as described on page 83

› Do not weave in any new elements but instead always cross over two elements of the same color, right over left, and secure with a clothespin.

› The structure will automatically become three-dimensional. There will be an octagonal hole in the center of the resulting basket.

› Continue to weave the side diagonally 1/1 and choose any rim solution you wish.

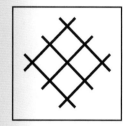 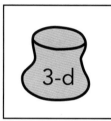

Basket made of saleen wicker with star-shaped base, diagonally woven 1/1

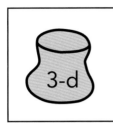
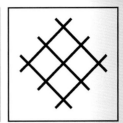
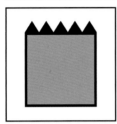
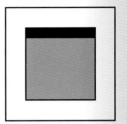

Materials

› Gift-wrapping paper about 76 × 56 cm (30 × 22 inches), in two colors

› 6 strips in each color, each 2 cm (0.8 inches) wide

› Cotton yarn scraps to secure the base

Prototype C: Case with rim of your choice

The paper version presented here is again a prototype, which is really easy to modify. A case has only two corners, not four like the baskets described above.

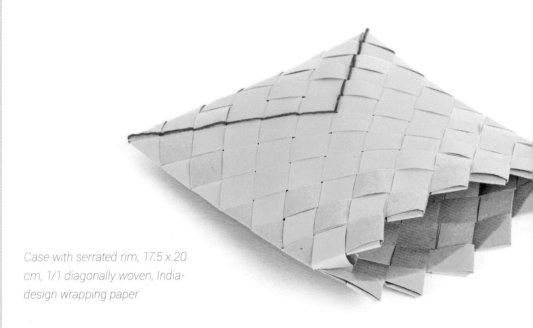

Case with serrated rim, 17.5 x 20 cm, 1/1 diagonally woven, India-design wrapping paper

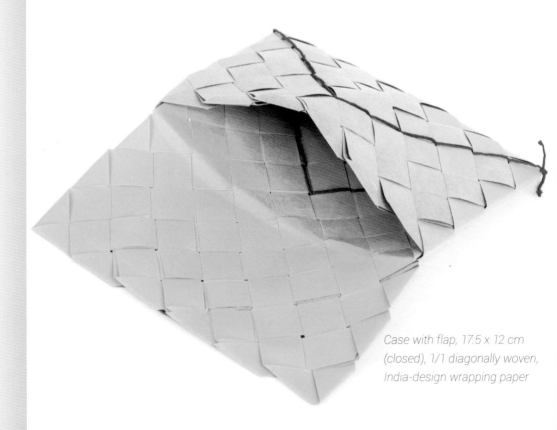

Case with flap, 17.5 x 12 cm (closed), 1/1 diagonally woven, India-design wrapping paper

1.

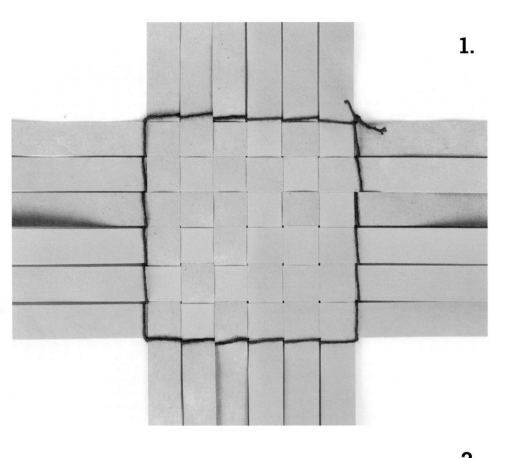

2.

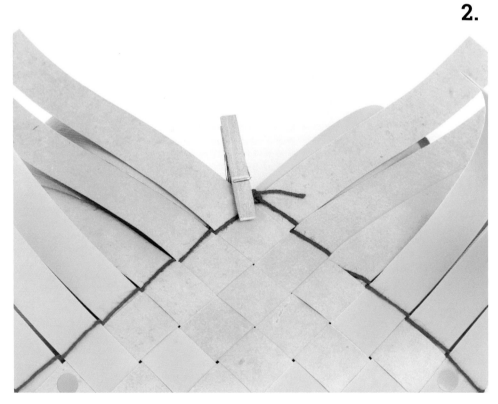

BOTTOM PIECE

› Weave a surface by using 6 x 6 elements, as done to make the base for the basket on page 135.
› Secure the surface with one round of twining. **[1]**
› Align the weaving elements to the same length.
› Fold the bottom piece as shown in figure 2. You now have a double triangle in front of you. Place the tips of the two triangles exactly on top of each other and secure with a clothespin. **[2]**

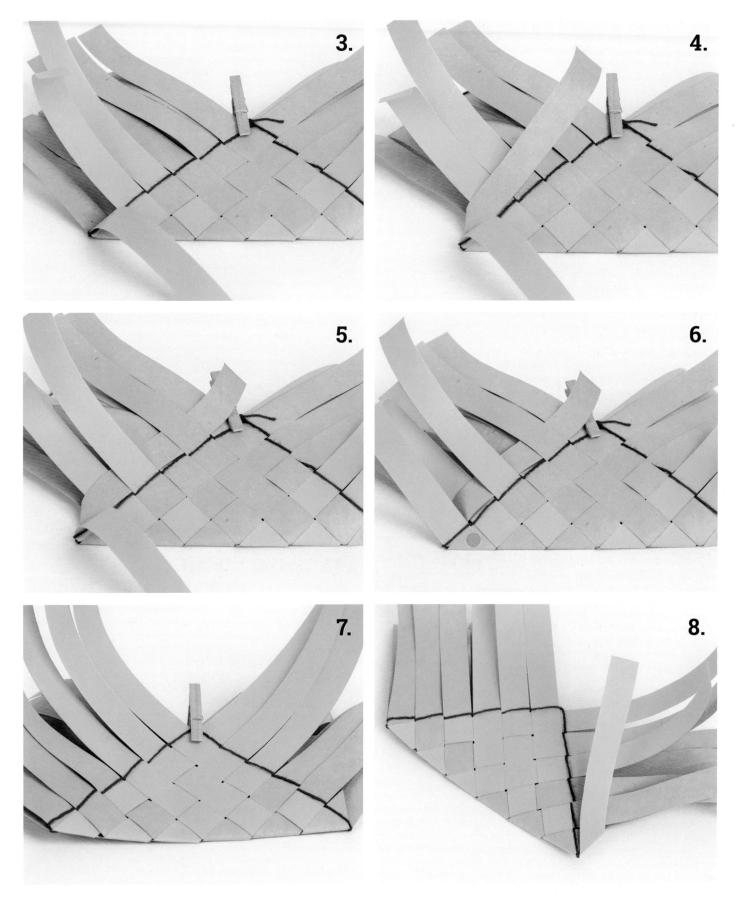

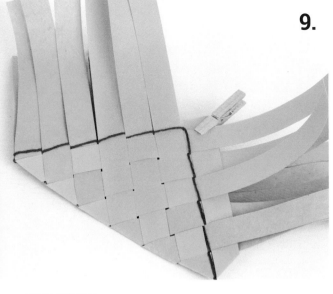

9.

Colorful case with inner case and flap,
1/1 diagonally woven

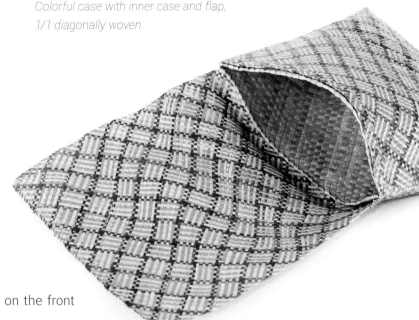

SIDE EDGES

To bind the two triangles together, work alternately once on the front side, then on the back side of the "triangle packet."

› Fold open the left yellow element on the upper triangle. **[3]**
› Fold the left blue element in the lower triangle on the left side over forward and align it parallel to the basting thread along the upper triangle. **[4]**
› Weave this strip in 1/1 pattern (you are weaving only with the elements in the upper triangle!). **[5]**
› Fold the left yellow element in the upper triangle back again. **[6]**
› Turn the piece. Now the side edge you started on is to the right. **[7]**
› Fold the right yellow element in the lower triangle on the left side over forward and align it parallel to basting thread along the upper triangle. **[8]**
› Weave this strip in 1/1 pattern (again, you are weaving only with the elements on the upper triangle!). **[9]**
› The game starts over again on the left side, starting from step 1. This time, you fold over a blue element first. Continue to work this way until the two triangles are completely interwoven together.
› Make sure that the resulting diagonal pairs are aligned at the same height while you are constructing the side edges. The higher the side edges grow, the shorter the paths for the weaving elements become.
› Inside the case, the edge created is completely straight, since all the elements will be folded over forward before the weave is started.

Variations

If you work it to a certain length, a case mutates into a tube with a round opening and flat starting section.

Tube-shaped
artifact from Zanzibar,
filled with spices; 2/2
diagonally woven in horizontal
twill; the starting section is sewn.

RIM

All sorts of finished edges are conceivable when making diagonally woven structures. If you have already woven a rim on the front side, keep on weaving the back surface and you will get a case with a flap. The flap becomes very thick and therefore stable because of all the end that you keep working back into the finished weave.

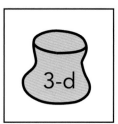
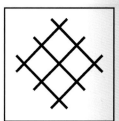

Prototype D: Bag with a narrow base

When making a diagonally woven basket, if you arrange the four corners on the bottom piece in a different way than was described above, you will get a very narrow base.

The starting point for the prototype described here is again a bottom piece of 6 x 6 interwoven elements (2 cm wide) made of yellow and blue wrapping paper. **[1]**

CORNERS AND SIDES

› Mark the future corners on the bottom piece as shown in figure 2. The corners you will make are right next to each other. **[2]**
› Shape the first corner as you learned to do when making prototype B. As you do so, be sure to maintain the correct 1/1 sequence for the woven elements. Secure with a clothespin. **[3]**
› Shape the second corner. **[4]**
› Shape corners 3 and 4 and weave the side. **[5]**

RIM

All sorts of finished edges are conceivable when making diagonally woven structures.

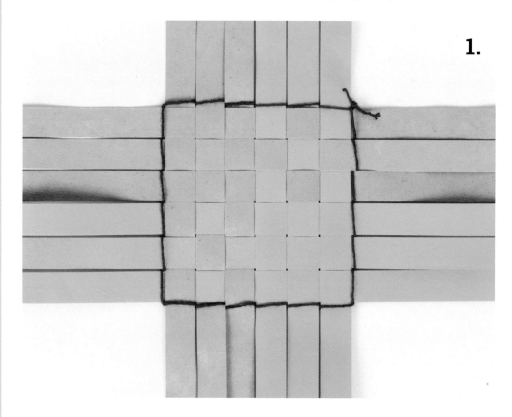

1.

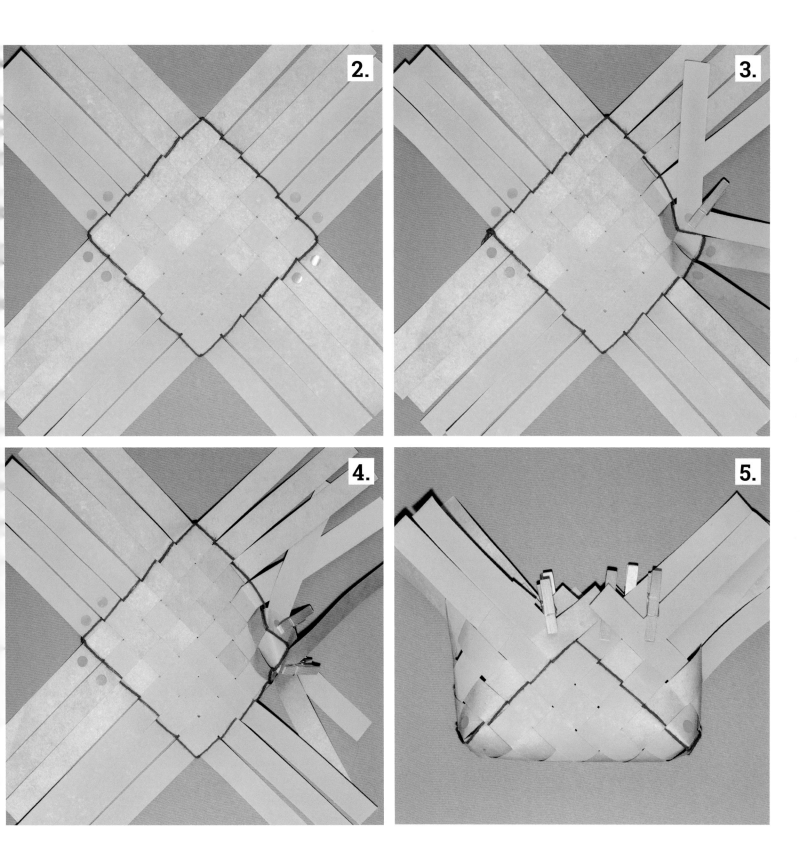

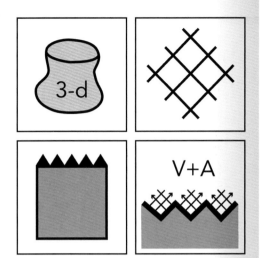

Materials

SnapPap is an interesting material—a leatherlike paper that is available in a wide range of colors. It is available in 50 × 150 cm (20 × 59 inch) sheets and should be washed and ironed before you work with it. This process shrinks the material a bit.

For a bag 30 cm (11.8 inches) wide and 39 cm (15.4 inches) high, you will need:

› 24 strips of SnapPap, each 2 cm (0.8 inches) wide and about 138 cm (54.3 inches) long. You will need one sheet.
› clothespins

If you follow these instructions, the weaving elements will be as long as you need right from the start, and it won't be necessary to lengthen them.

Bag with a narrow base made of vegan leather

This bag does not have a wide opening; it is suitable for holding a laptop, for example. It is woven like prototype D.

BOTTOM PIECE

› Weave a bottom piece of 10 x 10 strips. I worked from the center and, each time, slightly lifted up the elements that make the shed.
› Secure the bottom piece with one round of twining.
› Align the weaving elements to the same length.
› Make four corners as described for prototype D, and secure with clothespins.

SIDE

› When weaving the side, make sure that you always work in sections, as described on page 114. I interwove 5 x 5 elements together each time, going from the corner toward the right one time and going from the corner toward the left one time—which creates a nice zigzag working edge.
› Because the material is slippery, you should use plenty of clothespins. The beginning is a bit tedious, but when the structure becomes more compact after a few rows, it gets better and better.
› Before clipping on the clothespins, pay attention that the diagonal pairs meet at right angles.

RIM

This bag has a simple serrated edge (see page 126); you could just as easily make a straight finished edge. The shortest weaving element dictates when you have to bring all the elements to the same height to make the finished edge. The ends should be at least 8 cm (3 inches) long, so that you can work them back into the finished weave.

HANDLES

There are many possibilities for handles. Here we have bamboo bars with screwed-in metal crossbars. You could also choose a handle style using inserted cords or weave a tube (see page 161) from the strip remnants cut lengthwise in thirds (tube length about 50 cm) and machine-sew them to both sides of the bag. Or you can do without handles and attach a magnetic catch to the bag.

Vegan leather bag with handles and narrow base, 30 x 39 cm

Woven tubes as an option for the handles

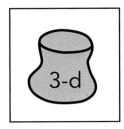 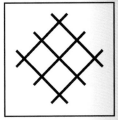

Materials

Saleen wicker, 2 cm (0.8 inches) wide, cut in half lengthwise, in two colors

For a tube with a diameter of about 2 cm (0.8 inches) and 28 cm (11 inches) long (without fringe), you will need:
› 1 strip in red, cut in half lengthwise, 1 meter (3.3 feet) long
› 1 strip in white, cut in half lengthwise, 1 meter (3.3 feet) long

Prototype E: Diagonally woven tube

This tube is woven completely freehand. Manioc presses (see page 23) or mysterious "finger trap" toys (see page 24) are made this way. Diagonally woven tubes are also used in medical technology, such as for stents or to set a broken finger bone.

Tube made of saleen wicker, diagonally woven

GETTING STARTED
› Weave two starting pieces from one red (half) and one white (half) strip, as described for the braid trim on page 102. **[1]**
› Interweave these two starting elements, as shown in figures 2 and 3. **[2 and 3]**

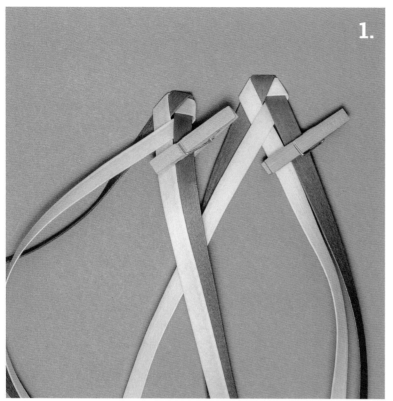

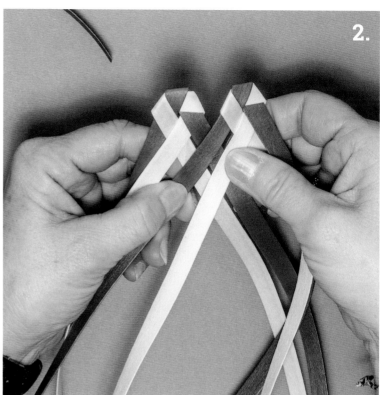

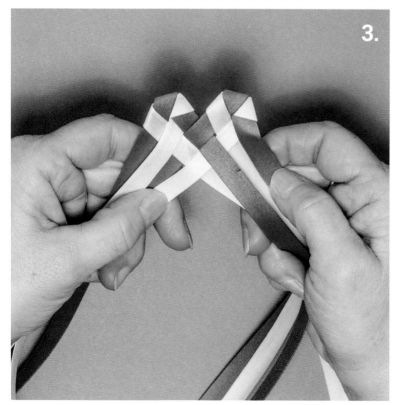

Test the sample by sticking your forefinger or thumb deep into the finger trap opening. Use your other hand to try to pull the finger trap off again. The only way to free yourself is to squeeze the tube by pushing in with your fingers. It's an example of the distinctive lengthwise and cross-wise elasticity of diagonally woven structures!

TUBE

› Take the work in your hands; you now have a group of diagonal Z elements on the left and a group of diagonal S elements on the right. It is essential that you always hold the strips of each group exactly right next to each other.

› Pass the right red S element, without twisting it, behind the piece on the left side and weave it 1/1 through the group of Z elements, as shown in figure 4. [4]

› The just-woven element has now moved from its place on the outermost rim to the place that is farthest inside the S group. [5]

› Pass the left-lying, loose Z element, without twisting it, behind the piece to the right side. [6]

› Then weave it into the S group [7 and 8], and as you do so, maintain the 1/1 sequence.

› This is how the piece looks from the back. [9]

› Keep on repeating these two rounds [10–12]. One time, the S element moves to the far right in the Z group on the left; one time the Z element on the far left moves to the S group on the right.

› After each two or three rounds, carefully pull on the weaving elements so that the weave is drawn together. You can leave the structure loose where you are currently working.

› Use scissors to trim the ends into a fringe and tie them together or weave them into a short plait.

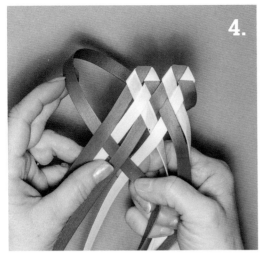

4.

Step 3 for weaving a tube

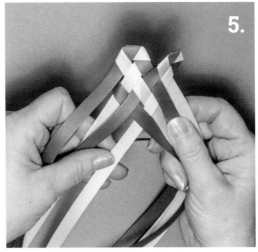

5.

New S and Z groups

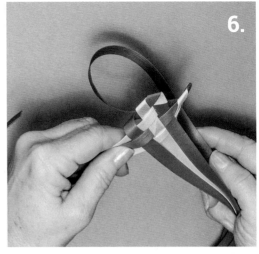

6.

Path for taking the loose Z element to the right

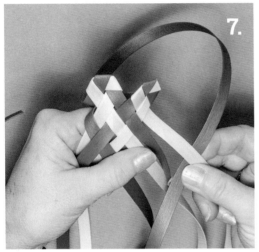

7.

Step 4 for weaving a tube

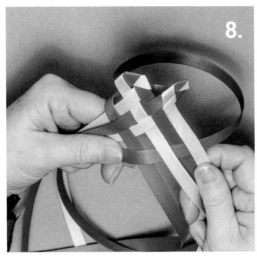

8.

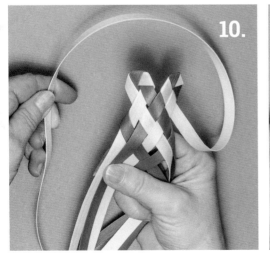

9.

View of the back of the resulting woven tube

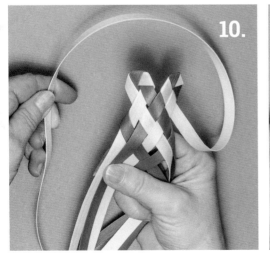

10.

Repeat step 3.

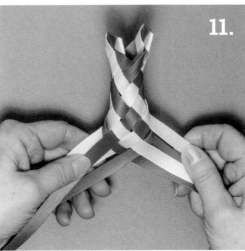

11.

Repeat step 4.

12.

View of the back of the resulting woven tube.

165

Materials

Soak 8 mm (3.2 inch) wide rattan cane (or flat rattan reed) in cold water for about 20 minutes and then wrap it in a wet cloth or in plastic. The rattan cane must be kept damp throughout the weaving process by using a wet sponge or spraying it by using a plant mister bottle, for example.

To make a 20 × 20 × 10 cm (8 × 8 × 4 inch) basket, you will need:

› 18 strips, each 48 cm (19 inches) long
› 5 strips, each 75 cm (29.5 inches) long
› fibers for binding the rims (I used paper cord)
› clothespins
› a sponge or spray mister

Objects Woven
in Three Directions

Prototype F: Open three-directional weave

This style of basket is made all over the world. Although it is woven in three directions and looks rather complex, it can be made relatively quickly and is not that difficult to weave. That may be one reason why this pattern is so widespread. On page 15, you can find a good example of how this weave is actually used.

The prototype presented here is woven of rattan cane. Cane and reed (cut from rattan stems) are available in craft stores and from basket-weaving suppliers. As an alternative, you can use any kind of stiff material, such as saleen wicker, veneer strips, photographic paper, and much more.

Basket woven in three directions in 1/1 pattern, rattan cane.

BASE

› Weave a base (equilateral hexagon) from the 18 strips as described on page 78. As you do so, keep the curved side of the rattan cane facing downward (the outside of the resulting basket). [1]
› You will get a hexagonal surface, woven in three directions, as well as six areas, each one with loose elements going in two diagonal directions. (Z-direction elements are underneath the S-direction ones.)
› Secure all six corners with clothespins, then moisten the work with water.

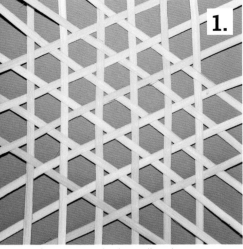

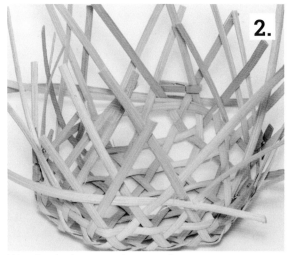

Bottom piece, woven in three directions

Weaving in the second extra splint

SIDE

You will need extra elements to construct the side. Here, these are the 75 cm (29.5 inch) long pieces of rattan cane, which were kept wrapped up until now.

› Mark the corner points of the base hexagon in pencil.
› Carefully bend upward all the (damp!) elements that run diagonally along the six side edges of the base ("upsetting"). The places where the two diagonals cross are close to the side edges of the base and turn upright in space ("upsetting"). Check whether all the Z elements are underneath the S elements.
› Start to weave in the first extra rattan cane at any point along the base side edge. The curved side of the cane is facing outward. This creates small, tightly 1/1 woven triangular areas. These are finished below the woven-in cane, but you are still constructing them above the cane. Close all the places above the cane so that the Z diagonal again lies underneath the S diagonal. You will notice that this already provides a very good support for the resulting structure.
› The start and the end of the woven-in extra elements overlap along a length of about 5 cm (2 inches). Secure with clothespins and moisten the work.
› The holes at the corners of the resulting basket are pentagonal and not hexagonal as in the rest of the structure.
› In figure 2, you can see how the second extra cane is woven in. **[2]**
› As you weave in the rest of the extra pieces of cane, check the shape of the resulting basket.

RIM

If the diagonal elements have become too short to allow you to weave in extra pieces of cane, make a finished edge by using extra elements as described on page 127.

Japanese-style basket, woven 1/1 in three directions, rattan splints, with freestyle rim and handles made of the remnants of the weaving elements

Open-weave covered baskets, bamboo, woven in three directions, Laos and Indonesia

A series of tetrahedrons made of saleen wicker

Enclosed Three-Dimensional Objects

As you shape these objects, the weaving elements close in on each other and thus come back to the starting point. You can layer the elements as much as you like. The structures can be both tightly and lightly woven. Nice examples of tightly woven, enclosed objects are the rattan balls on page 24. These objects have geometric shapes; they are cubes, tetrahedrons, or spheres.

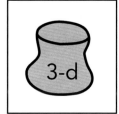
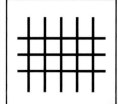
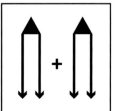

Orthogonally 1/1 woven cube

This cube is wonderful object for weaving with stiff materials, whether the cube is very small or very big. The prototype presented here is made of 2 cm (0.8 inch) wide saleen wicker.

Materials
Saleen wicker, 2 cm (0.8 inches) wide, in two colors
For a cube with an edge length of about 5.5 cm (2.2 inches), you will need:
› 1 strip in red, 1 meter (3.4 feet) long
› 1 strip in gray, 1 meter (3.4 feet) long
› clothespins

Variations
› Before weaving these objects closed, you can put items such as small bells inside them.
› Insert a key ring in the last layer.
› These closed objects are ideal for stringing together to make a decoration.

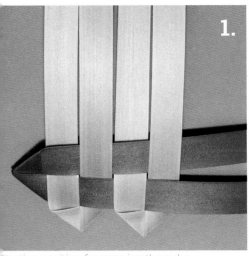

1.

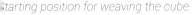
Starting position for weaving the cube

2.

Shape the first corner of the cube.

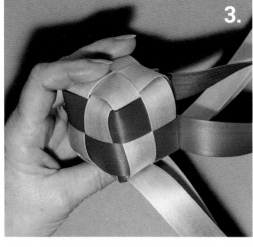

3.

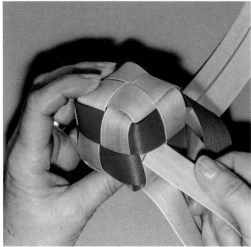
Keep working the ends back into the finished weave.

STARTING POSITION
› Fold each strip into one arrowhead.
› Weave the three arrowheads together as shown in figure 1. **[1]**

CONSTRUCTING THE CUBE SHAPE
› Weave the four gray elements 1/1 together as shown in figure 2, forming a corner and a small surface. Secure with a clothespin. **[2]**
› Now there are four elements next to each other on the right side, two gray and two red. Again weave a corner and a small surface, using the two middle strips of this row of four; secure with a clothespin.
› Now you have created a new group of four in your left hand. Use these to once more weave a corner and a small surface, using the two middle strips, and again secure with a clothespin. This has again created a group of four in your right hand. Make sure that the weaving elements are at right angles to each other.
› Use your left hand to bend the three tips of the starting elements toward the inside of the resulting cube.
› Use the last group of four to again weave the corner and the small surface. You have now woven the complete basic shape of the cube.
› Close the cube by weaving the loose weaving elements into the already woven surfaces of the cube. The weave now forms interwoven layers—doing this involves continuously working the ends back into the finished weave (**verstäten**). **[3]**
› Check to be sure you have made a uniform shape.
› The more often you keep weaving the elements over each other, the more compact and harder the cube becomes. Finally, trim all the ends.

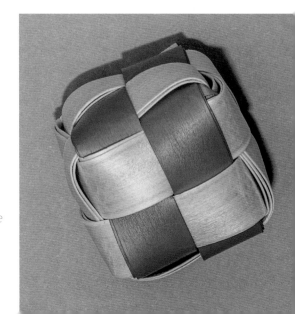
Orthogonally woven cube made of saleen wicker

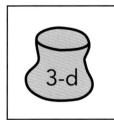
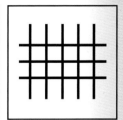
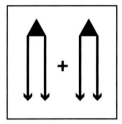

Materials

Saleen wicker, 2 cm (0.8 inches) wide, in two colors.

To make a tetrahedron with an edge length of about 10 cm (4 inches), you will need:

› 1 strip in red, 1.5 meters (5 feet) long
› 2 strips in gray, 1.5 meters (5 feet) long
› clothespins

Tetrahedron, 1/1 orthogonally woven

The tetrahedron looks as if it were woven both orthogonally as well as diagonally, but it is actually more of an orthogonal weave. The prototype presented here is made of 2 cm (0.8 inch) wide saleen wicker.

STARTING POSITION
› Fold each strip into one arrowhead.
› Weave the three arrowheads together as shown in figure 1. **[1]**

CONSTRUCTING THE TETRAHEDRON
› Bend the lower of the two red elements around the gray one and make a nick; this determines where the element will later lie in the weave. Let the element loose again.
› Hold the work in progress in your left hand and use the right hand to guide the weaving elements. Pass the upper red element in 1/1 pattern through the four gray elements, without swapping the top and bottom sides. **[2 and 3]**
› Draw the woven element tight and check all the angles. **[4]**
› Weave the other red element (with the nick) in 1/1 pattern through the four gray elements as shown in figure 5. **[5]**
› Draw this element tight and secure with a clothespin. **[6]** Now the two red elements are pointing to the left.
› Work using these elements exactly as you did before, but on the other side. Now your right hand is holding the piece, and your left hand is guiding the weaving elements. **[7–10]** Check each angle each time and draw the weaving elements tight. The two red elements are now pointing to the right again.
› Repeat the whole process once again. Pass the two red elements to the left again.
› Before passing these elements to the right again, bend the three tips of the starting elements toward the inside of the resulting artifact.
› Now weave the two red elements to the right again. The weave begins to form layers. Check the angles each time.
› First work the ends of the gray elements back into the first layer, then do this with the red ones. If you look at the structure carefully and if the angles are correct, you will be able see which paths the elements now have to take. Draw all the elements tight.
› The more often you keep weaving the elements over each other, the more compact and harder the tetrahedron becomes. **[11]**
› Finally, trim all the ends.

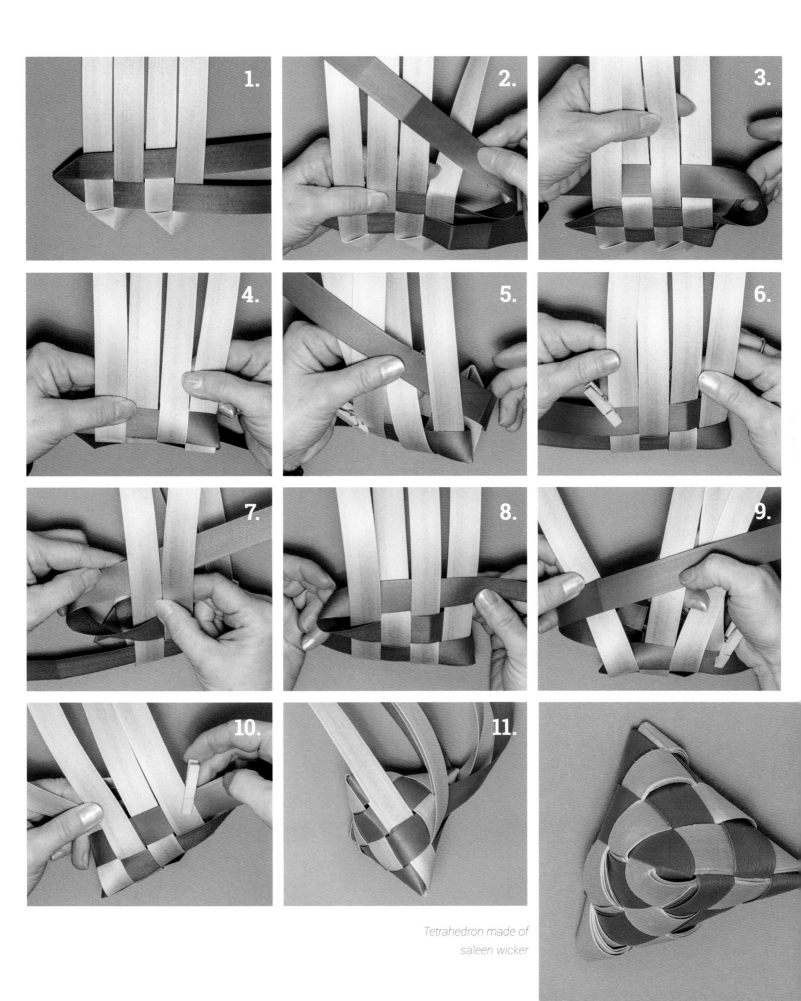

Tetrahedron made of
saleen wicker

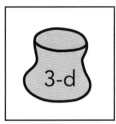
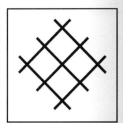
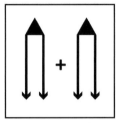

Materials

Saleen wicker, 2 cm (0.8 inches) wide, in two colors

To make a cube with edges about 4.5 cm (1.8 inches) long, you will need:
› 1 strip in red, 1 meter (3.4 feet) long
› 2 strips in gray, 1 meter (3.4 feet) long

Cube, 1/1 diagonally woven

A rather roundish cube is a beautiful object that works especially well when you use stiff materials. This prototype is made of 2 cm (0.8 inch) wide saleen wicker.

STARTING POSITION
› Fold each strip into one arrowhead.
› Weave the two arrowheads as when making the braid trim on page 95. **[1]**

CONSTRUCTING THE CUBE FORM
› Start by weaving a curling braid trim. However, keep the braid trim from curling to the left; steer the whole thing so that the braid trim is lying atop itself. **[2–4]**
› Bend the two arrowheads toward the inside of the resulting weave.
› Repeat the weaving steps to make a curling braid trim a few times until you can readily see how the weave is piling up. That will require about five rounds. Make sure that you are creating a consistent shape; the weaving elements should always be at right angles to each other.
› Then start to work the ends of the weaving elements back into the finished weave in a way consistent with the pattern of the already woven parts.
› The more often you keep weaving the elements over each other, the more compact and harder the cube becomes. **[5]**
› Finally, trim all the ends.

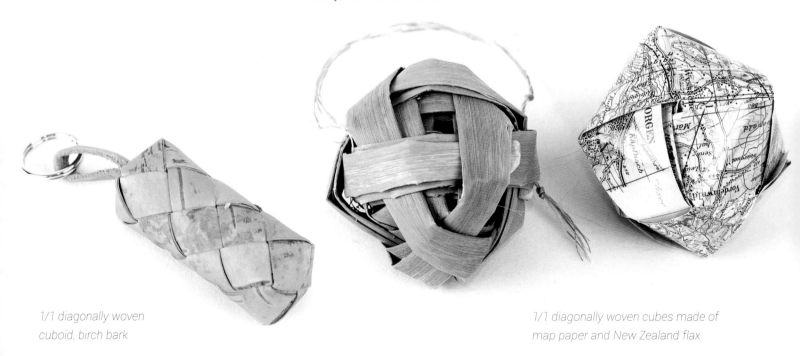

1/1 diagonally woven cuboid, birch bark

1/1 diagonally woven cubes made of map paper and New Zealand flax

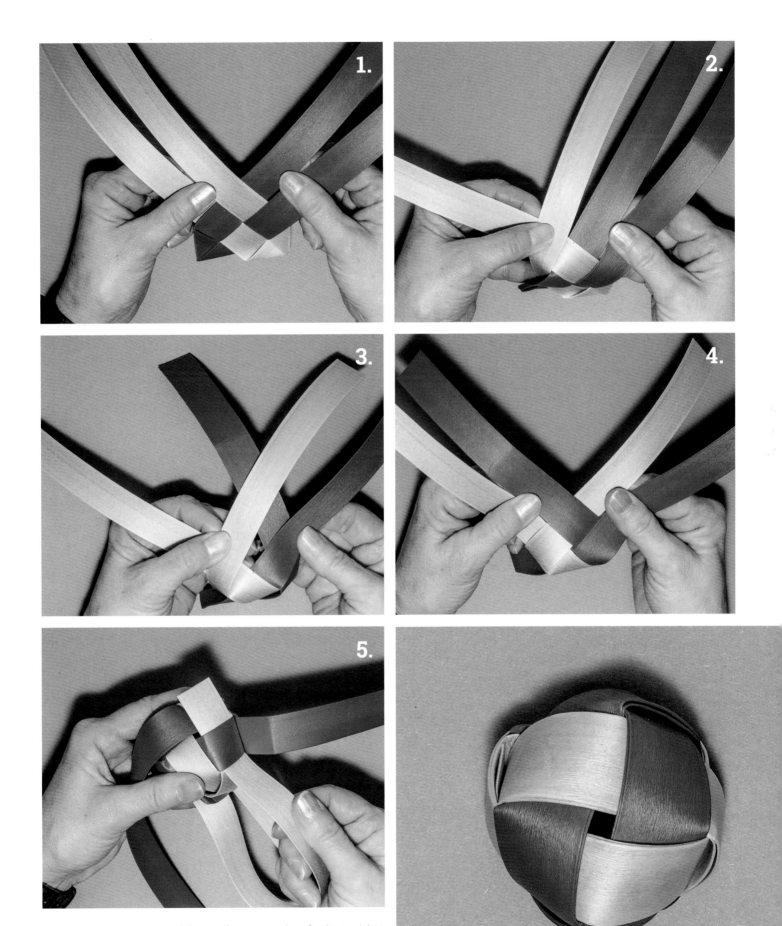

Diagonally woven cube of saleen wicker

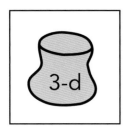 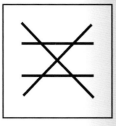

Open ball, woven in three directions

This is a genuine small miracle. You can weave a ball out of six equally long strips. It consists of 12 pentagonal holes and 20 equilateral triangles. If the holes were surfaces instead, you would get an icosidodecahedron.

Materials

It is essential to use stiff weaving elements, so that the woven object will curve out into the third dimension. Saleen wicker, heavy drawing paper, photographic paper, strips of veneer, flat rattan reed, and other such materials work well here.

Important: The ratio of the strip width to the strip length is about 1:20.

To make the sample shown here, you will need:
› 5 strips in gray, 2 cm (0.8 inches) wide and 40 cm (15.7 inches) long
› 1 strip in orange, 2 cm (0.8 inches) wide and 40 cm (15.7 inches) long
› clothespins

Large ball: thin paper board; small balls: saleen wicker

Modified into a ball-shaped basket

174

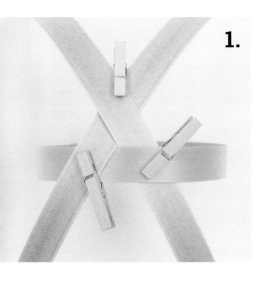

1.

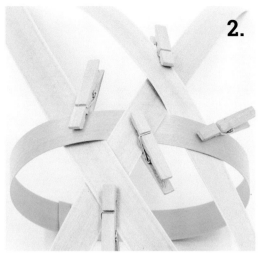

2.

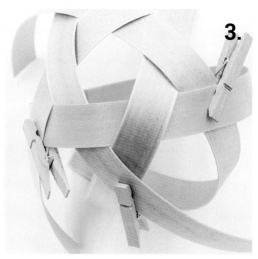

3.

CONSTRUCTING THE BALL

› Cut slots in both sides of each strip to make a slot connector (see page 49); these should be about 8–10 mm (3.2–4 inches) from the end of the strip.

› Join the orange strip ends into a ring.

› Weave two gray strips diagonally together along the orange ring as shown in figure 1. This will form a small, gray-orange, triangular surface (equilateral triangle with a 60-degree angle), which sits above the orange ring. Secure everything by using clothespins. **[1]**

› Using another gray strip, weave another gray-orange triangle to the left and underneath the orange ring, and secure it with clothespins. **[2]**

› Weave in another gray element as shown in figure 3. This forms a large pentagonal hole and a new gray-orange triangle on the orange ring. The piece will begin to curve outward. Secure the whole thing with clothespins. **[3]**

› Look for the spot above the first pentagonal hole, where the last gray element can be used to form another pentagonal hole with other already woven elements. Weave in the last strip, as shown in figure 4. **[4]**

› You can weave this strip in 1/1 pattern farther to the left and right, and the work will curve out even more. Do not add any new elements after that.

› Continue to make new pentagonal holes and tight triangles wherever you can. This will result in all the strips coming back to the place where they started. Use the slots already cut there to join the strip ends to make rings. Check to make sure that the sequence is really always kept as over 1/under 1 everywhere.

› Carefully tug on all the connectors under a gray triangle, so that the rings look nice and smooth.

4.

Ball, woven in three directions, with pentagonal holes

Patterns and Decorations

Two Groups of Patterns and Decorations

1. Patterns that are formed along with the structure of the weave

2. Patterns and decorations that are applied to the finished structure of the weave in a second step

The possibilities are endless. There is much that could be reported on here, especially in the cultural-historical and ethnological context: patterns not only beautify structures; they also serve to hand down stories and traditions and are of the greatest importance for many people. As the weaver creates the pattern, he or she applies an extraordinary level of craftsmanship, knowledge, and skill and an incredible imaginative power.

Round basket/sieve; origin: Brazil, Mato Grosso; materials: wood, plant splints, painted partially black on one side, twill weave; reinforced border: integrated wooden ring, woven over, cotton cord (Z twining) to make a loop on the rim. Ethnographic Museum at the University of Zurich, Inventory no. 06347a. Photo Kathrin Leuenberger

Twill pattern, orthogonally woven

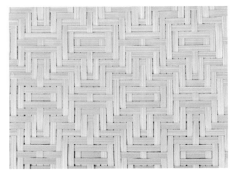

Detail of a place mat made of bamboo strips, twill pattern, orthogonally woven

Twill pattern, orthogonally woven, paper strips of slotted thin paper board

Twill pattern, orthogonally woven, printed wrapping paper

Structural Patterns

These emerge simultaneously with the weaving process; the following are potential ways to create patterns:

› varying the weaving rhythm such as over 1/under 1 combined with over 2/under 2
› using materials of different colors, such as strips of red and blue paper
› using different kinds of materials such as white strips of paper and white strips of plastic
› dividing the materials into narrower strips as you weave
› temporarily twisting individual weaving elements, forming patterns of holes
› making a curly or fringed design on the ends of weaving elements

TWILL PATTERN

This is likely the most popular and usual pattern that can be created during the weaving process. There are countless examples in museums, shops, and books. You can find monochrome, multicolored, orthogonal, and diagonal twill patterns. The weaving steps are always higher than 1/1; for example, 2/2 twill, 3/3 twill, and so on. Twill patterns appear as distinctive ribs or ridges/lines in the finished weave.

Twill patterns, orthogonally woven

Orthogonally woven twill patterns can be easily constructed along a straight starting line; for example, by using a row of arrowheads or simply using a row of lengthwise elements secured with adhesive tape. The cross-elements are woven in (with or without shedding) according to a counting pattern. Orthogonally woven twill patterns appear as diagonal ribs or ridges (as when weaving cloth). You can playfully design patterns on checkered paper; it is easy to transform these into the woven structure. Ready-made weaving reeds (school supplies) are also good for designing patterns.

Twill pattern, diagonally woven

Diagonally woven twill patterns are much more complex because these are created using the weaving elements already lying there.

A striking feature of all diagonally woven twill patterns is the distinctive ribs that are formed, either as lengthwise or crosswise ribs or a combination of these.

Detail of two-color twill patterning on a bag made in North Kalimantan, rattan strips, diagonally woven

Basket with high side, bamboo, diagonally woven, twill pattern with lengthwise and crosswise ribs, Bhutan

Detail of a bag made of New Zealand flax (Phormium tenax), 2/2 twill, diagonally woven with lengthwise and crosswise ribs

Vase-shaped basket; origin: Guatemala; diameter 15 cm, height: 18 cm, Ethnographic Museum at the University of Zurich, Inventory no. 24395a. Photo: Kathrin Leuenberger

Base section on a basket, virtuoso twill patterning, diagonally woven

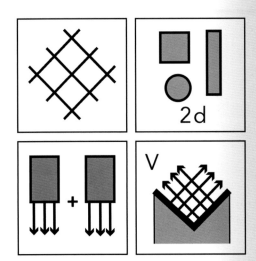

Twill pattern, 2/2 diagonally woven, based on a Polynesian style.

In her book *Baskets in Polynesia*, Wendy Arbeit writes about the methods, widespread throughout Polynesia, used to create twill patterns with what she termed "vertical twill" (lengthwise ribs) and "horizontal twill" (crosswise ribs). In these methods, four weaving elements are consistently interwoven to form a pattern in each work step. Saleen wicker is a good material for trying this out. Use 2 cm (0.8 inch) wide strips slit lengthways (do not cut completely through the wicker!). Work as follows:

> First, make a series of groups of strips as described on page 112; in the picture sample, there are three parcels of four elements each.
> A small V-shaped working edge is marked in the pictures. This is a key point: the four elements are interwoven along this working edge according to certain rules. To make both lengthwise and crosswise ribs, alternate two rows using different work steps.
> Lift up the four elements at a steep angle along the working edge to get a good view. Steer/guide two elements with each hand. **[1]**

Note: Figure 1 was taken when there was already progress in weaving the surface. The remaining pictures show situations when weaving the surface has just started.

CROSSWISE RIBS:

> You are working along a zigzag working line.
> In the center, you'll see a V-shaped working edge with two S and two Z elements (marked in black in figure 2). The left pair (the underlying one) is Z directed; the right is S directed. **[2]**
> Four S elements remain on the left and four Z elements on the right; these will be used later.
> When making crosswise ribs (after lifting all elements; see figure 1), the left Z pair is woven through the right S pair.
> When making crosswise ribs, you will alternate two different work series with each other.

Situation along the V-shaped working edge: lift up two elements at a steep angle with each hand.

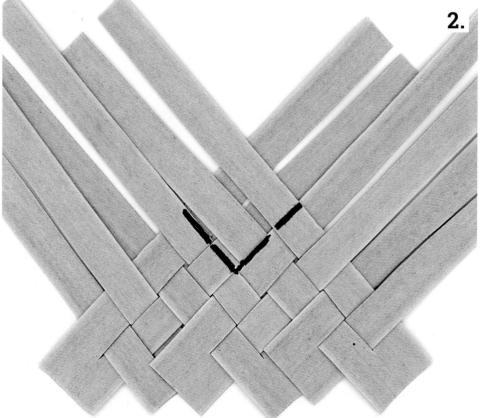

Starting position before lifting the elements

Weaving step for the first row:

› Pass the Z element lying closer to the V under the two S elements, and then the second Z element moves in under 1/over 1 pattern, through the S elements. **[3]**

› Secure with a clothespin. Important: you will not move these four elements again in this work series.

› Find the next group on the V-shaped working edge and work with them in exactly the same way.

› Turn as many elements along the side edges as you will need to again create groups of four along a V-shaped working edge.

› As shown in the arrangement in figure 2, using six S and Z elements each time, you will create three small woven surfaces at the end of the first row along the working edge—which is now A-shaped—as well as two new areas with V-shaped working edges.

Weaving step for the second row:

› In the second row, you will work along these new V-shaped working edges.

› The Z element that lies closer to the V moves over two S elements, and then the second Z element is woven, in over 1/under 1 pattern, through the S elements. **[4]**

› Secure with a clothespin. Important: you will not move these four elements again in this work series.

› Find the next group on the V-shaped working edge and work with them in exactly the same way.

› Turn as many elements along the side edges as you will need to again create groups of four along a V-shaped working edge.

› As shown in the arrangement in figure 2, you will create two small woven surfaces at the end of the second row along the working edge—which is now A-shaped—as well as one new area with a V-shaped working edge. Turn two elements each time along the side edges; this creates a total of three areas with V-shaped working edges.

› Keep on repeating rows 1 and 2; this will create distinct crosswise ribs in the growing structure. **[5]**

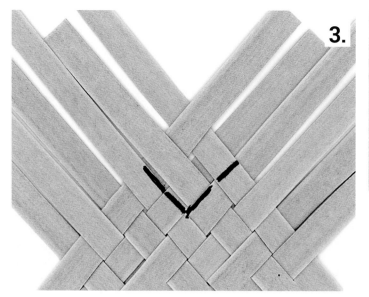

3.

Position of the elements after completing the weaving step in the first row

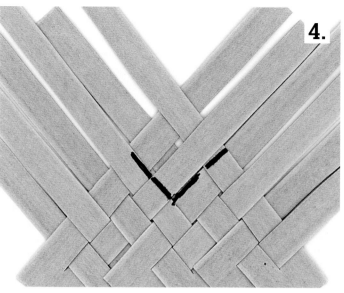

4.

Position of the elements after completing the weaving step in the second row

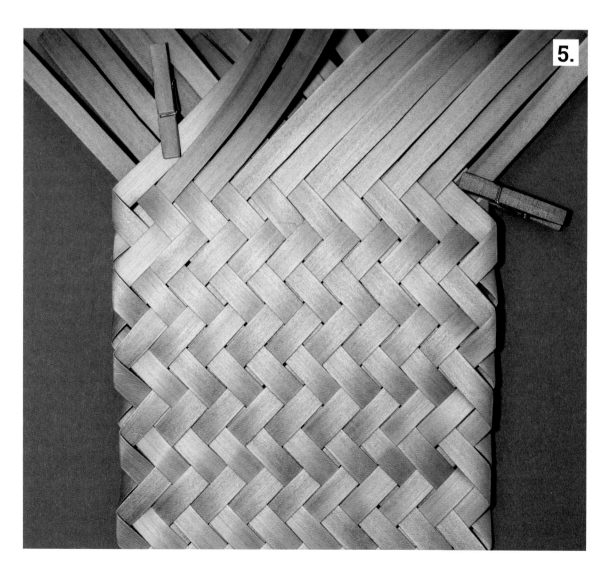

5.

Twill pattern, diagonally woven, crosswise ribs, saleen wicker

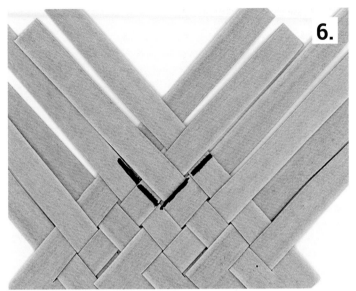

Position of the elements after completing the weaving step in the first row

Position of the elements after completing the weaving step in the second row

LENGTHWISE RIBS:

› You are working along a zigzag working line.
› In the center, you'll hav a V-shaped working edge that has two S and two Z elements (marked in black in figure 2). The left pair (the underlying one) is Z directed; the right is S directed. [2] (figure 2; see page 181)
› Four S elements remain on the left and four Z elements on the right; these will be used later.
› To make lengthwise ribs, the right-hand S pair is woven through the left-hand Z pair.
› When making lengthwise ribs, you will alternate two different work series with each other:

Weaving step for the first row:

› The S element closer to the V moves over two Z elements, then the second S element is woven, in under 1/over 1 pattern, through the Z elements. Secure with a clothespin. [6]
› Find the next group on the V-shaped working edge and work in exactly the same way.
› Turn as many elements along the side edges as you will need to again create groups of four along a V-shaped working edge.
› As shown in the arrangement in figure 2, using six S and Z elements each time, you will create three small woven surfaces at the end of the first row along the working edge—which is now A-shaped—as well as two new areas with V-shaped working edges.

Weaving step for the second row:

› In the second row, you will work along these new V-shaped working edges.
› The S element lying closer to the V moves under two Z elements, and then the second S element is woven, in over 1/under 1 pattern, through the Z elements. Secure with a clothespin. [7]
› Weave the entire row in this way, and turn as many elements along the side edges as you will need to again create groups of four along a V-shaped working edge.
› As shown in the arrangement in figure 2, you will create two small woven surfaces at the end of the second row along the working edge— which is now A-shaped—as well as one new area with a V-shaped working edge. Turn two elements each time along the side edges; this creates a total of three areas with V-shaped working edges.
› Keep on repeating rows 1 and 2; this will create distinct lengthwise ribs in the growing structure. [8]

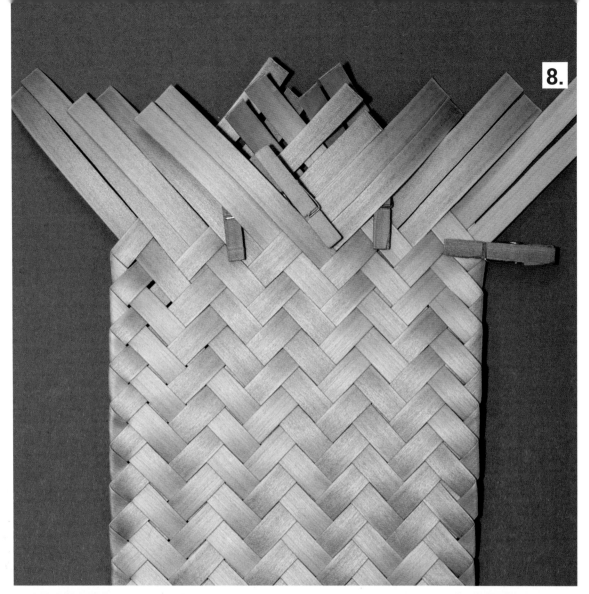

Twill pattern, diagonally woven, lengthwise ribs, saleen wicker

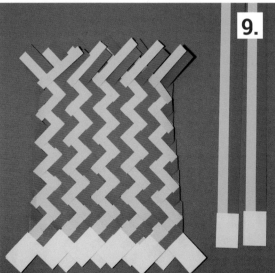

Woven in two colors, crosswise ribs look like zigzag lengthwise strips.

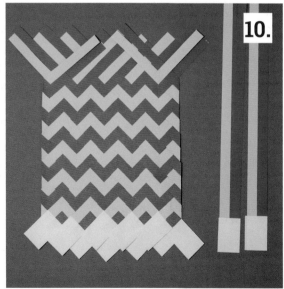

Woven in two colors, lengthwise ribs look like zigzag horizontal strips.

<u>Notes:</u>

› Shaping the edges of the flat piece is very tricky work: pay close attention to how you have to turn the elements so that the weaving pattern is the correct 2/2.

› Working in rounds, however, is enjoyable. It is necessary that the number of weaving elements is divisible by four.

› If this is combined with colored weaving elements, amazing things happen. **[9 and 10]**

Patterns with **Colored Weaving Elements**

The color pattern that is created in the weave is already determined as you start weaving. You can experiment or plan on a piece of checkered paper—try it out!

Here you see an example of how to create a windmill pattern in a 1/1 diagonally woven mat:

› Use sticky labels to make two groups of the yellow strips and two groups of the green strips, each time grouping 2 x 2 strips of the same color (see page 112).
› Fasten the groups of strips together along the side, while alternating the colors of the groups. Weave 4 x 4 strips together, always section by section, as described on page 113.
› Pay careful attention along the rims and side edges.
› This builds up a windmill-like pattern, which is especially striking if there is a significant light-dark contrast between the strip parcels.

It is also fun to weave a colorful design without using any particular pattern—surprises are guaranteed!

Experiment using yellow and green strips.

Mat in two-color pattern, 1/1 diagonally woven, tissue paper and sewing pattern paper, folded over four times

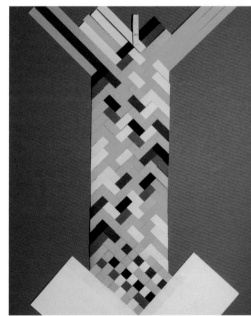

Freestyle color combination

Vividly colored baskets at a market in Bali. Photo: Christian Muehlethaler

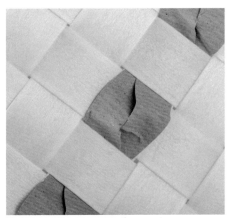

Detail of a bag from the Solomon Islands, pandanus, pattern made using strips woven in afterward, 1/1 and twill, diagonally woven

Patterns and Decorations
Applied After Weaving

These patterns are not created by the weaving process but are applied to the weave only after it is finished. There are many ways to do this.

Weaving a pattern into a finished structure

This is a very simple and efficient way to create a pattern and decorate a piece. You can follow the original weave design or not. Patterning is very often created by using colored strips. This makes the patterns look as if they had been woven directly into the basic structure.

WOVEN-IN RAISED PATTERN

Some of the attractive variations of weaving patterns into a finished structure include the bobble-like raised pattern and curling decorations often found on woven pieces from Southeast Asia. You can easily try this yourself:
> Working on a 1/1 woven structure will be especially easy!
> You need two strips per row; these should be about 1–2 mm (0.4–0.8 inches) narrower than the weaving strips used for the basic structure.
> Place both strips together, one atop the other, and fasten them into the basic weave.
> Cross the two strips once, such as the right strip over the left, and then again place the strips back together, one exactly atop the other.
> In the weaving rhythm, pass the strips, one atop the other, under one element in the finished structure, then pull them through and cross them again. Then again place the strips together, one exactly atop the other.
› Continue to work in this way. The two strips will bulge into a bobble-like raised pattern on top of the weave.

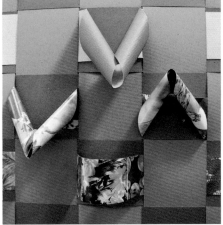

Raised pattern made of wrapping paper on saleen wicker

WOVEN-IN CURLS
To do this, weave individual strips into the finished structure:
> Fasten the starting strip into the weave.
> Turn the strip once around itself and hold it fast in this position.
> Turn the strip once again in the opposite direction before passing it under an element in the finished structure.

Woven-in curls and bands

Embroidering a finished structure

If you want to add extra elements to one of the finished edges, as explained on page 127, a good way to attach them is to use embroidery stitches. The small holes in a weave of strips make it easy to pull a needle and thread along their pattern-forming path through the finished weave. If you need to pierce the weaving materials, you will also need an awl and a suitable pad. When embroidering, you can also attach other decorative elements such as shells, seeds, or pearls.

Imprinting or inscribing a finished structure

The surface of a weave of strips is often flat and smooth enough for you to inscribe it or print on it. This method makes it possible to apply even complicated patterns, which would not work if you used just weaving techniques alone. Even the simplest stamps or stencils create interesting results. You can also inscribe the weave by using wide pens.

The creation of patterns by using printing techniques is a broad field of research in ethnology.

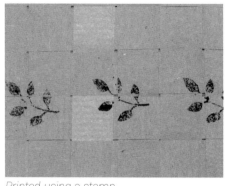

Printed using a stamp

Money mat (front), plant fibers, pigments, Pentecost Island, Vanuatu, Felix Speiser collection, before 1912, ©Vb4435, Museum der Kulturen Basel. Photo: Peter Horner, 1983

Conclusion

I couldn't possibly tell you everything about structures woven of strips of material—there is still so much to discover! And I would not be surprised if, after reading this book, you would be able recognize strips in all sorts of places and see them with completely new eyes!

LEGEND

Finally, a little story from Hawaii from the book by A. Bird, S. Goldsberry, and P. Bird: The Craft of Hawaiian Lauhala Weaving:

Of the many Polynesian legends about the sky, there is one of interest for lauhala weavers.

It is said by some that night came when a large, tightly woven basket made by the gods was placed over the islands.

Opposite page: view from a diagonally woven basket of lime woodchip

The stars were sunlight shining through the tiny holes in the weave.

Even today, basket weavers examine the quality of their work by placing baskets over their heads. If the holes are as small as stars, the weavers know they have done a good job.

04

The Pictograms and Their Meaning

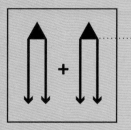

Folded arrowhead elements

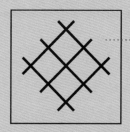

Arrowhead and weft element

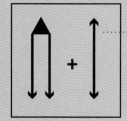

Elements integrated at the base

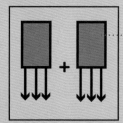

Two-dimensional objects

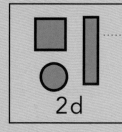

Three-dimensional object

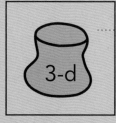

Orthogonally woven

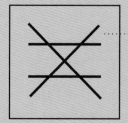

Diagonally woven

Woven in three directions

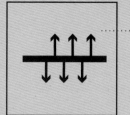

Woven in four diretions

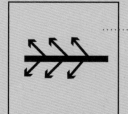

Horizontal working edge

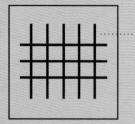

Cross-grain working edge

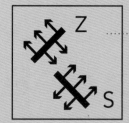

Straight-grain working edge, S or Z directed

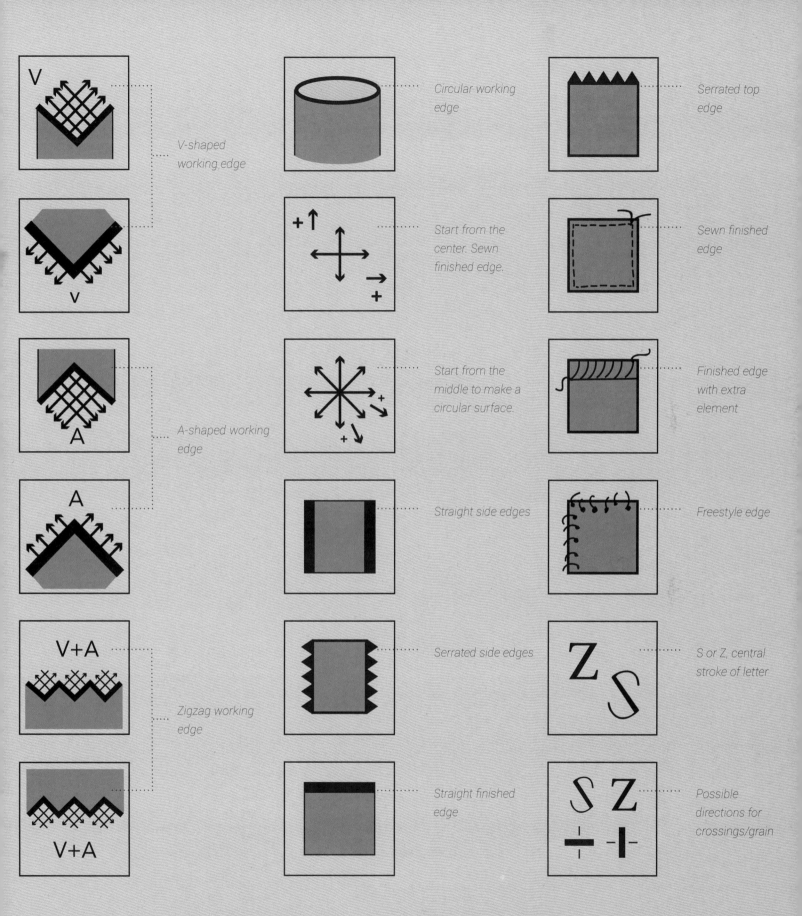

V-shaped working edge

Circular working edge

Serrated top edge

A-shaped working edge

Start from the center. Sewn finished edge.

Sewn finished edge

Start from the middle to make a circular surface.

Finished edge with extra element

Straight side edges

Freestyle edge

Zigzag working edge

Serrated side edges

S or Z, central stroke of letter

Straight finished edge

Possible directions for crossings/grain

Appendix

Sources

The following sources are fundamentally important for my work:

WORKS ON CLASSIFICATION OF TEXTILES

General remarks on the classification of textile structures

There are two fundamentally different ways to analyze and classify textile structures:
1. according to the manufacturing process
2. according to the texture and appearance

Neither of these methods says anything about historical, geographical, social, cultural, and art-historical developments —you are simply analyzing the objects, and either you inquire as to how they were made, or you describe their texture and structure.

The "Basel classification system" (*Systematik der Textilen Techniken*)— classification according to the manufacturing process or technique

This is the first classification system that I learned about at the Museum der Kulturen Basel.

Organization into four main sections:
1. the techniques for making threads or fibers
2. the techniques for making fabric
3. the techniques for decorating fabric
4. the techniques for processing fabric

The second section, "The techniques for making fabric," is the one relevant for me. This is subdivided into

a) primary fabric-making techniques (no or only a few aids and tools)
b) more advanced fabric-making techniques (some complicated aids and tools)
The topics covered in this book belong to 2a.

Classification according to Noémi Speiser

This classification has yet to be published. For me, this is the most descriptive one I know. The focus is clearly on the manufacturing process and on the work process. During our many years of collaboration, Noémi Speiser's analytical and systematic thinking has greatly influenced me.

Organization into three main categories/super-categories:

I. working with a single thread or fiber
II. working with a set of threads or fibers
III. working threads or fibers into an already prepared set of threads or fibers

The super-categories can be subdivided into subcategories, down to the individual case.

The majority of weaving techniques presented in this book belong to the second and third super-categories.

LITERATURE ON BASKETRY
Noémi Speiser and her book *The Manual of Braiding*

This fundamental book was first published in 1983 and deals with bands and braid trims—diagonally woven structures (from super-category II; see above)—mostly made of materials with a round cross section. Working with this book made me realize how diversified and interesting even a single technique group can be. Among the sample pieces woven from strips, I discovered the clever method of folding a strip over forward or backward and the principle of using arrowheads.

Fortunately, this out-of-print book is now available again from Haupt Verlag as a reprint.

Peter Collingwood and his book on textile structures

This book gave me some "aha" moments and provided many ideas for products! It first appeared under the title *Textile and Weaving Structures* in 1987 and was published in German in 1988 under the title *Textile Strukuturen: Eine Systematik der Techniken aus aller Welt (Textile Structures: Classification of Techniques from All over the World*) by Haupt Verlag in German (now out of print). This book is convincing not only because of its well-founded information on manufacturing techniques and materials used to make textile artifacts, but also because of its references to the respective applications and the people who made or used the artifacts.

Although this book is not an instruction book in the true sense of the word, its excellent picture material and the clear sketches of individual structural details help with self-educational tinkering.

Johannes Lehmann and his *Systematik und geographische Verbreitung der Gelechtsarten (Classification and Geographical Distribution of Types of Weaving).*

This is the oldest German-language classification system that I have found so far. It mainly deals with weaves and knots. Johannes Lehmann published this work in 1907. The structures are presented in a sophisticated mathematical formula system (which I tried unsuccessfully to fathom) and supplemented with plates of pictures and drawings. I found it interesting that in dealing with weaving elements, Lehmann distinguishes between weaving strands and weaving strips; that is, whether the material has a round or flat in cross section.

Peter Buck and his ethnographic books

When I started my research in the mid-1990s, the university libraries provided me with valuable information from their ethnological and ethnographic materials. I came across the books of Peter Buck, whose Maori name was Te Rangi Hīroa. He was an important specialist in the cultural techniques from Oceania and Polynesia and illustrated his research on weaving techniques with very detailed drawings that were a great help to me for trying things out and experimenting.

Jack Lenor Larsen and Betty Freudenheim and their book *Interlacing: The Elemental Fabric*

I kept carrying this long-out-of-print book home from the library for years and then finally was able to buy it from a used bookstore in 2011. With its pictures, tables, and drawings, it is a key work for my own research and experimenting. Unfortunately, in German, we do not have any exact translation for the fabulous English word "interlacing"; the approximate German translation is *verschränken* (used for folding your arms or crossing your legs).

Literature on basket weaving

As I'm a trained basket and basketwork designer, of course all books about basket weaving are interesting sources for me. However, these rarely contain anything about my favorite techniques for using strip-like materials.

And I enjoy exchanging ideas with professional colleagues from all over the world, which has become so easy thanks to the internet!

OTHER SOURCES
Museums and exhibitions

In museums that focus on history, folklore, and ethnology and in exhibitions, I keep discovering, again and again, objects that give me insight into the structures or manufacturing processes using in primary fabric-making

techniques. It is worth checking whether there are accessible libraries, depositories, or study collections in museums. You will find addresses below.

The Internet

The internet is a good source of information today—if you are aware that not everything that can be found on the World Wide Web is true! YouTube films with working instructions have now become very popular.

Suggestions for search terms:
» prehistoric and early historical textiles
» archeological textiles
» weaving
» basket weaving
» mat weaving
» ketupat
» twill woven
» plaiting techniques
» mathematische-basteleien.de (mathematical-crafting.de)

Artists in the basketry field (selection)
» Bacon, Laura Ellen
» Bundesinnungsverband des deutschen Flechthandwerks, flechtwerkgestalter.de (German National Guild for Basketry Handicraft basketrydesigners.de)
» Butcher, Mary
» Drury, Chris
» Fisch, Arline M.
» Gill Barnes, Dorothy
» IGK SCHWEIZ korbflechten.ch (Interessengemeinschaft Korbflechterei Schweiz: Basket Weavers Interest Group Switzerland basketweaving.ch)
» Jamart, Susan
» Laky, Gyöngy
» Linder, Margrit
» Moore Bess, Nancy
» O'Sullivan, Annemarie
» Odon (Guy Houdouin)
» Pet Lamps, petlamp.org
» Rossbach, Ed
» Schmid, Franz R.
» verein flechtwerk, flechtwerk-ev.de (Basket Weaving Association basketweaving-reg. assn.de)
» Westphal, Katherine

» Zentrum europäischer Flechtkultur Lichtenfels, flechtkultur.eu (Center for European Basket Weaving, Lichtenfels, Germany basketweavingculture.eu)

Sources for objects
» flea markets
» secondhand stores
» estate sales
» museum shops and world shops
» the internet

BIBLIOGRAPHY (SELECTION)

Araseki, Mayumi. *eco craft*. Tokyo: Little Bird, 2013.

Arbeit, Wendy. *Baskets in Polynesia*. Honolulu: University of Hawai'i Press, 1990.

Arndt, Ingo. *Architektier (Animal Architecture)*. Munich: Knesebeck Verlag, 2015.

Ashley, Clifford W. *The Ashley Book of Knots*. Boston and London: Faber & Faber, 1993.

Bird, Adren J, Steven Goldsberry, and J. Bird. Puninani Kanekoa: *The Craft of Hawaiian Lauhala Weavin*g. Honolulu: University of Hawaii Press, 1982.

Buchet, Martine. *Panama: Chapeau de Légende (Panama: The Legendary Hat)*. Paris: Editions Assouline, 1995.

Bühler-Oppenheim, Kristin, and Alfred Bühler-Oppenheim. *Grundlagen zur Systematik der gesamten textilen Techniken (Fundamentals for Classification of All Textile Techniques)*. Basel, Switzerland: Memoranda of the Schweizerischen Naturforschenden Gesellschaft (Swiss Society of Natural Sciences), vol. LXXVIII, treatise 2, 1948.

Butcher, Mary. *Contemporary International Basketmaking*. London: Merrell Holberton, 1999.

Collingwood, Peter. *Textile Strukturen: Eine Systematik der Techniken aus aller Welt (Textile Structures: Classification of Techniques from all over the Worl*d). Bern and Stuttgart: Haupt Verlag, 1988.

Collingwood, Peter. *The Maker's Hand: A Close Look at Textile Structures.* London: Bellew, 1987, 1998.

Dendel, Esther Warner. *African Fabric Crafts: Sources of African Design & Technique.* New York: Taplinger, 1974.

Deutsches Korbmuseum Michelau (German Basket Museum, Michelau). *Begleitbuch zur Dauerausstellung (Companion Book to the Permanent Exhibition). Schriften des Deutschen Korbmuseums Michelau (Writings of the German Basket Museum Michelau)* 2, 1994.

Emery, Irene. *The Primary Structures of Fabrics.* Washington, DC: Thames & Hudson, 1966.

FEDEAU (Fedération pour le Dévéloppement de l'Artisanat Utilitaire [Federation for the Development of the Utility Craft Industry]). *Vannerie du Monde (World Basketry).* Paris, 1980.

Fisch, Arline M. *Textile Techniken in Metall (Textile Techniques in Metal).* Bern and Stuttgart: Haupt Verlag, 1988.

Gliszczynski, Vanessa von, Mona Suhrbier, and Eva Ch. Raabe, eds. *Der rote Faden: Gedanken Spinnen Muster Bilden (The Common Thread: The Warp and Weft of Thinking).* Bielefeld, Germany: Kerber Verlag, 2016.

Grant, Bruce. *Encyclopedia of Rawhide and Leather Braiding.* Centerville, MD: Cornell Maritime, 1972.

Harvey, Virginia I. *The Techniques of Basketry.* New York: Van Nostrand Reinhold, 1974.

James Cook und die Entdeckung der Südsee (James Cook and the Discovery of the South Seas) (exhibition catalog). Zurich: Verlag Neue Zürcher Zeitung, 2009.

Jensen, Elizabeth. *Korbflechten: Das Handbuch (Basket Weaving: The Handbook).* Bern and Stuttgart: Haupt Verlag, 1994.

Knöpfli, Hans. *Grasland: Eine afrikanische Kultur (Grassland: An African Culture).* Wuppertal, Germany: Peter Hammer Verlag, 2008.

Kobayashi, Keiko. *From Thread to Fabric.* Tokyo: Nichibou Shuppan Sha, 2013.

Küchler, Susanne, and Graeme Were. *Pacific Pattern.* London: Thames & Hudson, 2005.

Kuhn, Dieter, Anton Wohler, Marcela Hohl, Marcela, and Birgit Littmann. Strohzeiten. *Geschichte und Geschichten der aargauischen Strohindustrie (Straw Times: History and Stories of the Aargau Straw Industry).* Aarau, Germany: AT Verlag, 1991.

LaPlantz, Shereen: *The Mad Weave Book.* New York: Dover, 1984.

Lang-Harris, Elizabeth, and Charlene St. John. *Hex Weave & Mad Weave.* Atglen, PA: Schiffer, 2013.

Larsen, Jack Lenor, and Betty Freudenheim. *Interlacing the Elemental Fabric.* New York and Tokyo: Kodansha International, 1986.

Lehmann, Johannes. *Systematik und geographische Verbreitung der Geflechtsarten (Classification and Geographical Distribution of Types of Weaving).* In *Abhandlungen und Berichte des Königl. Zoologischen und Anthropologisch-Ethnographischen Museums zu Dresden (Treatises and Reports of the Royal Zoological and Anthropological Ethnographic Museum of Dresden).* Leipzig: Teubner, 1907.

Maihi, Toi Te Rito, and Maureen Lander. *He Kete He Korero: Every Kete Has a Story.* Auckland, New Zealand: Reed, 2006.

Main, Veronica. *Zauberhaftes Stroh: Herstelltechniken aus dem Freiamt (Magical Straw: Manufacturing Techniques from the Freiamt Region).* Bucks, UK: Main Collins, 2003.

Marks, Andreas. *Modern Twist: Contemporary Japanese Bamboo Art.* Washington, DC: International Arts & Artists, 2012.

McGuire, John. *Basketry: The Shaker Tradition.* New York: Lark Books, 2004.

Mellgren, Jette. *Flechten mit Naturmaterial (Weaving with Natural Materials).* Stuttgart: Freeh Verlag, 2011.

Pendergrast, Mick. *Fun with Flax.* Auckland, New Zealand: Reed, 2007.

Pendergrast, Mick. *Māori Fiber Techniques.* Auckland, New Zealand: Reed, 2005.

Pendergrast, Mick. *Te Mahi Kete: Māori Flaxcraft for Beginners.* Auckland, New Zealand: Reed, 2000.

Rast-Eicher, Antoinette, and Anne and Dietrich. *Neolithische und bronzezeitliche Gewebe und Geflechte (Neolithic and Bronze Age Fabrics and Weaves).* Monographien der Kantonsarchäologie Zürich (Monographs of Zurich Cantonal Archeology) 46. Zurich, 2015.

Ribalta, Marta, ed. *Volkskunst Amerikas (American Folk Art).* Bern and Stuttgart: Hallwag Verlag, 1981.

Rossbach, Ed. *Flechtkunst (Baskets as Textile Art).* Ravensburg, Germany: Otto Maier Verlag, 1979.

Rossbach, Ed. *The Nature of Basketry.* West Chester, PA: Schiffer, 1986.

Rowe, Ann Pollard, and Rebecca A. T. Stevens. Ed Rossbach: *40 Years of Exploration and Innovation in Fiber Art*. Washington, DC: Lark Books, 1990.

Schindlbeck, Markus, ed. *Von Kokos zu Plastik: Südseekulturen im Wandel (From Coconut to Plastic: South Sea Cultures in Transition)*. Berlin: Dietrich Reimer Verlag, 1993.

Seiler-Baldinger, Annemarie. *Systematik der Textilen Techniken (Classification of Textile Techniques)*. Basler Beiträge zur Ethnologie (Basel Contributions to Ethnology) 32. *Basel: Ethnologisches Seminar der Universität und Museum für Völkerkunde, (Ethnology Seminar of the University and Museum of Ethnology)*, commissioned by Wepf AG Verlag, 1991.

Sellato, Bernard, ed. *Plaited Arts from the Borneo Rainforest*. Honolulu: University of Hawai'i Press, 2012.

Sennett, Richard. *Handwerk (Handicrafts)*. Berlin: Berliner Taschenbuch Verlag, 2009.

Sentance, Bryan. *Atlas der Flechtkunst (Atlas of Basketry)*. Bern and Stuttgart: Haupt Verlag, 2001.

Speiser, Noémi. *The Manual of Braiding*. Self-published, 1991; Reprint, Bern and Stuttgart: Haupt Verlag, 2018.

Stiftung Freiämter Strohmuseum Wohlen (Freiamt Straw Museum Foundation), eds. *Freiämter Strohmuseum Wohlen (Freiamt Straw Museum)*. Trimbach, Germany: Nord-West-Druck, 1995.

Ströse, Susanne. *Werken mit Palmblatt und Binsen (Works Made with Palm Leaves and Rushes)*. Munich: Don Bosco Verlag, 1966.

Sudduth, Billie Ruth. *Korb-Design: Inspirationen und Projekte (Basket Design: Inspirations and Projects)*. Bern and Stuttgart: Haupt Verlag, 2001.

Takamiya, Noriko, Tsuruko Tanikawa, and Kazue Honma. *Basketry*. Tokyo: Nihon Vogue-Sha, 1998.

Textil: Technik Design Funktion (Textiles: Technique Design Function). Basel: Museum der Kulturen (Museum of Cultures), 2000.

Thode-Arora, Hilke. *Weavers of Men and Women*. Berlin: Dietrich Reimer Verlag, 2009.

Verdet-Fierz, Regula, and Bernard Verdet-Fierz. *Anleitung zum Flechten mit Weiden (Instructions for Willow Basket Weaving)*. 2nd ed. Bern and Stuttgart: Haupt Verlag, 2004.

Westfall, Carol, and Suellen Glashausser. *Plaiting Step-by-Step*. New York: Watson-Guptill, 1976.

Will, Christoph. *Die Korbflechterei (Basket Weaving)*. Munich: Callwey Verlag, 1978.

World Art Collections Exhibition, Sainsbury Centre for Visual Arts. *Basketry: Making Human Nature*. Norwich, UK: University of East Anglia, 2011

MATERIALS SUPPLIERS (SELECTION)

Germany
Paper, paper strips:
» www.buttinette.com
» www.modulor.de
» www.origami-papier.eu
» www.boesner.com
» www.gerstaecker.de

Paper tape:
» www.finnische-papierschnur.de
» www.webgarne.de

Flat rattan reed, rattan cane, straw plaits, saleen wicker:
» www.schardt-kg.de
» www.hans-ender.de

Vegan leather/SnapPap:
» www.snap-pap.de

Austria

Flat rattan reed, rattan cane, straw:
» www.dieroff.at

Paper:
» www.boesner.at
» www.gerstaecker.at

Vegan leather/SnapPap:
» www.stoffschwester.at

Switzerland

Tape:
» www.tressa.ch

Craft woodchip, felt tape, cork tape, leather strips, straw stalks:
» www.leibundgutag.ch

Paper, paper strips:
» www.bauundhobby.ch
» www.leibundgutag.ch
» www.boesner.ch
» www.gerstaecker.ch

Paper tape:
» www.webkante.ch

Flat rattan reed, rattan cane:
» www.leibundgutag.ch
» www.peddig-keel.ch

Saleen wicker:
» www.fehrerlen.ch
» www.peddig-keel.ch

Straw plaits:
» www.getreidedeko.ch

Vegan leather/SnapPap:
» www.arpagaustextil.ch

Japan

Paper tape (wrapfun):
» https://global.rakuten.com/en/store/
wrapfun

MUSEUMS (SELECTION)
Auckland War Memorial Museum
Auckland Domain, Parnell, Auckland, New
Zealand
www.aucklandmuseum.com

Bernice Pauahi Bishop Museum, 1525
Bernice Street, Honolulu, HI 96817, www.
bishopmuseum.org

Bernisches Historisches Museum (Bern
Historical Museum), Einsteinmuseum
(Einstein Museum), Helvetiaplatz 5, 3005
Bern, Switzerland, www.bhm.ch

British Museum, Great Russell Street,
London, GB-WC1B 3DG, www.
britishmuseum.org

Ethnologisches Museum Berlin
(Ethnological Museum of Berlin), www.
smb.museum Ethnologisches Museum
Berlin, www.smb.museum (Currently
closed, reopening in the Humboldt Forum
in late 2020.)

Grassi-Museum für Völkerkunde zu
Leipzig (Grassi Ethnology Museum in
Leipzig), Johannisplatz 5–11, 04103
Leipzig, Germany, https://grassi-
voelkerkunde.skd.museum

Laténium, parc et musée d'archéologie de
Neuchâtel (Neuchâtel Acheological Park
and Museum), Espace Paul Vouga, 2068
Hauterive, Switzlerland, www.latenium.ch

Linden-Museum Stuttgart, Staatliches
Museum für Völkerkunde (State Musuem
of Ethnology), Hegelplatz 1, 70174
Stuttgart, Germany, www.lindenmuseum.
de

Musée du quai Branly, 37 Quai Branly,
F-75007 Paris, www.quaibranly.fr

Museum am Rothenbaum, Kulturen und
Künste der Welt (Museum of World
Culture and Art), Rothenbaumchaussee
64, 20148 Hamburg, www.markk-
hamburg.de

Museum der Kulturen (Museum of
Cultures) Basel, Münsterplatz 20, 4001
Basel, Switzerland, www.mkb.ch

Museum der Strohverarbeitung (Museum
of Straw Plaiting), Kapellenweg 2, 27239
Twistringen, Germany, www.
strohmuseum.de

Museum Fünf Kontinente (Museum of
Five Continents), Maximilianstraße 42,
80538 Munich, www.museum-fuenf-
kontinente.de

Museum für Archäologie und Ökologie
Ditmarschen (Museum of Archeology and
Ecology of Ditmarschen,) Bahnhofstraße
29, 25767 Albersdorf, Germany, www.
museum-albersdorf.de

Museum für Völkerkunde Dresden
(Museum of Ethnology Dresden),
Japanisches Palais, Palaisplatz 11, 01097
Dresden, https://voelkerkunde-dresden.
skd.museum

Museum of New Zealand Te Papa
Tongarewa, 55 Cable Street, Wellington
6011, New Zealand, www.tepapa.govt.nz

Museum Rietberg, Zurich, Gablerstrasse
15, 8002 Zurich, www.rietberg.ch

Strohmuseum im Park (Straw Museum in
the Park), Bünzstrasse 5, 5610 Wohlen
AG, Switzerland, www.strohmuseum.ch

Textilmuseum St. Gallen (St. Gallen
Textile Museum), Vadianstrasse 2, 9000
St. Gallen, Switzerland, www.
textilmuseum.ch

Tropenmuseum Amsterdam,
Linnaeusstraat 2, 1092 CK Amsterdam,
www.tropenmuseum.nl

Übersee-Museum Bremen (Overseas
Museum Bremen), Bahnhofsplatz 13,
28195 Bremen, Germany, www.uebersee-
museum.de

Völkerkundemuseum der Universität
Zürich (Ethnological Museum of the
University of Zurich), Pelikanstrasse 40,
8001 Zurich, www.musethno.uzh.ch

Weltmuseum Wien (Museum of
Ethnology, Vienna), Heldenplatz, 1010
Vienna, www.weltmuseumwien.at

Index

A

Arrowheads, 84, 85, 86, 89, 90, 92, 93, 94, 95, 96, 98, 100, 107, 118, 121, 124, 169, 170, 172, 178, 194

B

Basel classification system 35, 194
Basket, 12, 13, 14, 15, 18, 35, 39, 51, 52, 55, 70, 131, 133, 134, 135, 136, 138, 144, 145, 147, 148, 149, 150, 152, 153, 166, 167, 177, 179, 191, 195, 197, 200
Basting thread, 46, 82, 100, 115, 134, 136, 147, 152, 157
Bracelet, 27, 142
Braid trim, 39, 58, 74, 86, 89, 90, 93, 94, 95, 96, 97, 98, 102, 104, 105, 106, 107, 110, 122, 142, 162, 172
Buck, Peter, 111, 195
Bundled ends, 110

C

Classification system, 8, 35, 194, 195, 196, 197
Collingwood, Peter, 194, 196
Cramming-spacing effect, 37, 38, 108, 147
Crossing, 76, 82
Curls, 188

D

Diagonal, 16, 17, 18, 19, 22, 23, 24, 26, 30, 36, 3 7, 38, 51, 52, 53, 54, 55, 58, 76, 93, 94, 95, 96, 98, 100, 104, 106, 108, 110, 112, 114, 115, 117, 118, 120, 126, 130, 131, 133, 138, 144, 145, 149, 150, 151, 152, 153, 154, 157, 158, 162, 164, 167, 170, 172, 175, 178, 179, 180, 183, 185, 186, 188, 191, 194

E

Enclosed objects, 39, 168

F

Fabric, 35, 36, 59
Fabric-making technique, 194
Fiber connections, 34
Fiber or thread, 34, 35, 36, 45, 58, 67, 136, 140, 189, 194, 196
Finished edge, 50, 84, 100, 119, 120, 121, 122, 123, 127, 134, 136, 149, 160, 167, 193
Fold, 43, 59, 70, 84, 86, 92, 95, 96, 98, 102, 112, 121, 122, 127, 169, 170, 172
Four directions, 38, 82, 192
Freudenheim, Betty, 195, 196

G

Growth direction, 49

H

Hexagonal, 80, 167

L

Larsen, Jack Lenor, 8, 195
Lehmann, Johannes, 195, 196
Lengthen, 43, 47, 49, 65, 114, 134, 136, 138, 144, 149, 150, 152, 160
Leutwyler, 4, 8
Linder, Margrit, 4, 14, 15, 17, 22, 28, 29, 40, 47, 51, 76

M

Mat, 12, 20, 21, 22, 28, 29, 38, 39, 40, 54, 86, 89, 90, 92, 108, 111, 114, 186
Museum der Kulturen Basel, 4, 8, 9, 23, 111, 194, 198

O

Orthogonal, 12, 16, 19, 21, 23, 27, 28, 36, 37, 47, 52, 54, 57, 70, 75, 76, 82, 86, 90, 107, 108, 115, 117, 118, 133, 134, 135, 138, 141, 142, 145, 168, 170, 178

P

Pentagonal holes, 175
Phormium tenax, 42, 105, 179
Plait, 39, 58, 164

R

Raised pattern, 140, 188
Rattan, 9, 17, 19, 22, 24, 26, 28, 29, 38, 51, 53, 76
Row, 67, 107, 121, 124, 127, 178, 180, 182, 183, 184, 188
Round, 65, 66, 67, 70, 134, 138, 145, 149, 153, 155, 160, 149, 153, 155, 160

S

S-directed, 35, 37, 104, 180, 184
Schmid, Franz R., 4, 30, 31
Shedding, 35, 36, 38, 66, 70, 134, 136, 145, 149, 178
Slot connector, 49, 175
Speiser, Noémi, 4, 8, 38, 194
Splint, 55
Strips, 8, 9, 20, 23, 35, 39, 40, 41, 42, 43, 44, 45, 46, 48, 49, 52, 54, 55, 60, 61, 64, 66, 70, 76, 78, 82, 84, 86, 89, 90, 94, 95, 96, 98, 102, 104, 107, 108, 110, 112, 134, 136, 138, 144, 147, 148, 149, 152, 153, 154, 157, 160, 162, 164, 166, 168, 169, 170, 172, 174, 175, 178, 186, 188, 189, 191, 194
Structure, 25, 34, 35, 37, 39, 50, 51, 52, 53, 65, 76, 80, 81, 82, 92, 100, 106, 119, 138, 147, 153, 160, 164, 167, 170, 177, 178, 182, 184, 188, 189, 194

T

Tape, 173
Textile technique, 35
Thread or fiber, 34, 35, 36, 45, 58, 67, 136, 140, 189, 194, 196
Three directions, 19, 24, 38, 74, 78, 102, 106, 122, 128, 166, 167, 174, 175, 192
Tightly woven, 39
Tool, 46
Tube, 102, 136
Turn, 35, 45, 48, 100, 138
Turn (rotate), 48
Twill pattern, 16, 18, 19, 22, 23, 26, 47, 55, 100, 133, 178-185
Twining, 66, 67, 134, 138, 145, 149, 155, 160 199 145, 149, 155, 160
Two directions, 37, 38, 66, 82, 122

V

*Verstäten (*working the ends back into the finished weave), 51, 95, 120, 121, 122, 123, 124, 126, 127, 134, 142, 169, 170, 172, 124, 126, 127, 134, 142, 169, 170, 172

W

Weave (noun), 12, 24, 35, 37, 38, 39, 41, 47, 49, 51, 52, 54, 56, 59, 66, 67, 70, 78, 82, 84, 85, 89, 92, 94, 96, 100, 110, 111, 112, 118, 119, 120 , 121, 122, 123, 124, 126, 127, 128, 134, 138, 140, 142, 149, 151, 157, 164, 169, 170, 172, 178, 186, 188, 189
Weave (verb), 13, 21, 29, 30, 35, 36, 41, 42, 43, 49, 52, 60, 64, 6 7, 80, 96, 100, 104, 122, 124, 134, 147, 149, 150, 152, 155, 157, 169, 175, 197, 200
Weaving element, 34, 51, 67, 94, 100,104, 150, 160
Weaving pattern, 36, 58
Weaving step, 36, 6 7, 94, 119, 127, 138, 182, 184
Weaving techniques, 8, 12, 13, 18, 21, 27, 30, 34, 37, 39, 52, 64, 189, 194, 195
Working line, 36, 38, 49, 120, 126, 180, 184
Working edge, 36, 38, 39, 49, 76, 84, 86, 89, 90, 93, 94, 96, 98, 100, 104, 110, 112, 114, 118, 120, 147, 148, 160, 180, 181, 182, 184, 192, 193
Working the ends back into the finished weave (*verstäten*), 51, 95, 120, 121, 122, 123, 124, 126, 127, 134, 142, 169, 170, 172, 124, 126, 127, 134, 142, 169, 170, 172
Woven together, 58, 111, 114

Z

Z-directed, 34, 35, 37, 76, 121, 180, 184

About the Author

My knowledge comes from years of self-educated learning, a basic study of ethnology, and an apprenticeship as a designer of baskets and of basketry. I search curiously for new horizons in the thousands-of-years-old textile techniques that do not need a loom. For me, there are two main issues in this process: the interlinking and intertwining techniques and basket weaving. What fascinates me is the way the under and over of the individual elements creates a connection—in all directions and in any spatial dimensions you wish. First, I explore and try out the traditional work methods and then experiment with my own ideas: what all is possible to achieve, including by using uncommon materials and unconventional interpretations of weaving techniques.

www.flechtwerk.ch

Acknowledgments

Without those well-known relationship threads (networking is also a textile discipline!), this book could not have been created. I thank Adela and Matthias Haupt and their publishing team for their confidence in my topics. My thanks go to Heidi Müller, Eva Hauck, and Christina Diwold for their competent support, the careful editing, and the design of the book. And I especially want to warmly thank Samuel Künti for the outstanding photographic material—without these fabulous pictures, a book of instructions would have been simply "indigestible." A big thank-you goes to all the innumerable course participants over the past years—their feedback is enormously important to me. For additional picture materials, I would like to thank Margrit Linder; Prof. Dr. Mareile Flitsch, Dr. Alexis Malefakis, and Kathrin Kocher at the Museum für Völkerkunde (Museum of Ethnology), Zurich; Josef Gisler of the Kantonsarchäologie Zürich (Zurich Cantonal Archaeological Institute); Dr. Beatrice Voirol, Doris Kähli, and Regina Mathez at the Museum der Kulturen Basel (Basel Museum of Cultures); Anna Hegi at the Strohmuseum im Park (the Straw Museum), Wohlen, Switzerland; Christine Zbinden; Christian Mühlethaler; Anna Sonderegger; Franz R. Schmid; and Peter Santschi.

And last but not least, I thank Hans Künti for his patient computer support—without him, I would have very often become hopelessly lost.